MY FATHER'S RIFLE

HINER SALEEM

MY
FATHER'S
RIFLE

A CHILDHOOD IN KURDISTAN

Translated from the French by Catherine Temerson

FARRAR, STRAUS AND GIROUX
New York

Farrar, Straus and Giroux
19 Union Square West, New York 10003

Library of Congress Cataloging-in-Publication Data
Saleem, Hiner, 1964–
    [Fusil de mon père. English]
    My father's rifle : a childhood in Kurdistan / Hiner Saleem ;
translated from the French by Catherine Temerson.— 1st American ed.
    p.   cm.
    ISBN-13: 978-0-374-21693-1
    ISBN-10: 0-374-21693-2 (hc. : alk. paper)
    1. Saleem, Hiner, 1964–   2. Kurds—Iraq—Biography.   I. Title.

DS70.8.K8S25313 2005
956.7'204'092—dc22
[B]

                                                        2004047127

Designed by Debbie Glasserman

www.fsgbooks.com

1   3   5   7   9   10   8   6   4   2

MY FATHER'S RIFLE

My name is Azad Shero Selim. I am Selim Malay's grandson. My grandfather had a good sense of humor. He used to say he was born a Kurd, in a free country. Then the Ottomans arrived and said to my grandfather, "You're Ottoman," so he became Ottoman. At the fall of the Ottoman Empire, he became Turkish. The Turks left and he became a Kurd again in the kingdom of Sheikh Mahmoud, king of the Kurds. Then the British arrived, so my grandfather became a subject of His Gracious Majesty and even learned a few words of English.

The British invented Iraq, so my grandfather became Iraqi, but this new word, *Iraq*, always remained an enigma to him, and to his dying breath he was never proud of being Iraqi; nor was his son, my father, Shero Selim Malay. But I, Azad, I was still a kid.

Seated under the big mulberry tree in the garden of our beautiful old house, my mother was seeding pomegranates. I could see only the tip of her flowery scarf. The pulp from the seeds colored her hands and her face was stained with the red juice of the autumn fruit.

Me, I was squatting on my heels, stuffing myself. My mother handed me the best seeds and kept repeating, "My son, go change your shirt," for I was wearing my white school shirt. Having eaten my fill, I stood up when I heard the fluttering of wings in the sky. It was my cousin Cheto's stunt pigeons. I went down to our orchard and slipped under the barbed wire that ran around it. I climbed up the ladder to the rooftop of my cousin's house, the rooftop where we were in the habit of sleeping during the summer. There I joined Cheto and his three cages of trained pigeons. My cousin proudly showed me the pigeon he was holding in his hands, then he tossed it toward the sky. The bird took flight, soared up into the blue sky, then plummeted like a deadweight in the void and began whirling about itself. We were fascinated and we watched the pigeon, spellbound. When the performance ended, he flew in a wide circle over our heads, then landed next to us. This was my cousin's champion stunt pigeon, and he called it Lion. Cheto took a second pigeon and tossed it toward the sky. The spectacle was just as beautiful but at the end the pigeon didn't come back and we lost sight of it. We went down into the orchard and each walked in an opposite direction to look for the pigeon. I was sure the pigeon hadn't landed in a cherry tree, but I scanned the treetops just in case. Suddenly I heard very agitated voices, right next to our house, in back of the orchard. This was not normal.

I started running to see what was happening. I inched my way under the barbed wire and my shirt got caught. While I was trying to free myself, I heard the cries of terrified women. Perhaps someone had died? I lunged forward and my white school shirt ripped.

When I reached the back of the house, I saw my mother come out, distraught, grasping the Koran wrapped in its green cloth. She held it out toward tense armed men. In a shaken voice, she screamed at them, "For the love of the

Koran, don't touch my house." Right before my eyes, she was hit with the butt of a rifle and collapsed to the ground. My mother was on her knees, trying to get to her feet. When she saw me, she shouted to me, terrified, to go hide—for a male, whether a child or a grown-up, could be killed. I rushed toward her, but she pushed me away as she stood up and I ran to the orchard to hide behind a tree. I heard gunshots everywhere in our neighborhood. People were screaming. Smoke and fire rose from our house. I was aghast and fascinated. From behind my tree, I saw other armed men arrive. They were looking for Mamou, a cousin. His house had already been reduced to ashes.

Mamou was thirty years old and a schoolteacher. Every Friday, at prayer hour, Mamou minded his father's dry-goods store while his father, a prominent Aqra shopkeeper, was at the mosque. On that day, about ten men from Omar Akha's pro-government militia entered the shop. Mamou was a sympathizer of General Barzani, leader of the Kurdish patriots.★ The militiamen began taunting my cousin, who remained calm until their leader called him a coward and a Barzanist cuckold. At that point, without saying a word, Mamou went to the back of the store and pulled out a 9 mm revolver buried under rolls of fabric; then, returning to face the militiamen, he said just one word, "*djache*," collaborator, and fired three shots straight into the militia leader's head. After that, he killed two other militiamen and managed to escape. It was clear they had come to kill him, and he wanted to die like a man.

When he got to the front of his house, he didn't go inside, to avoid being trapped. Keeping an eye on the street, he called out to his mother and asked her to bring him his rifle. The militiamen were getting closer while my cousin

★Mullah Mustafa Barzani, leader of the Kurdish Democratic Party, who had been military leader of the Kurdish Republic in Iran in 1946. —Translator's note

waited for his rifle and all his bullets. But my aunt, panic-stricken, had misunderstood and thought she was supposed to hide the rifle, so she didn't come out of the house. My cousin could do nothing but run away, his pistol his only weapon. In passing through our neighborhood, the militia-men had killed my uncle Rasul, Cheto's father. Mamou headed for the nearby hills with the militiamen hot on his heels. He hid behind a rock to try to bandage a wound. Then he was surrounded, and shots were fired on all sides. My cousin defended himself to the last bullet. When his magazine was empty, he was caught alive. But they didn't execute him. They came down from the hills, tied his feet to the back of a jeep with a rope, and dragged him to the town. Three times they drove him around the town center, as a warning to the other patriots. By then my cousin was a life-less rag streaked with blood.

That day, we lost seven men in our family. We fled.

I was still a kid.

My family arrived in Billē filled with a tremendous desire for revenge. Billē was a small village of about a hundred homes not far from Raizan, the town where the leader of our peo-ple, Mustafa Barzani, had his headquarters. This was the sec-ond time I had left my hometown of Aqra. The first time, my mother had taken me far away to pay my father a visit. He had just been released from jail and was living under house arrest in the middle of the desert, on Iraq's southern border with Saudi Arabia. My father was accused of having stolen a Morse code transmitter for the Kurdish movement.

Billē was located on the bank of the Zab River, a large tributary of the Tigris. The entire right bank was controlled by the *peshmergas*,★ Kurdish fighters. From the first day we

★Literally, "he who looks death straight in the face." —Translator's note

arrived, a one-room house was put at our disposal by order of General Barzani himself.

Our neighbors brought us large trays laden with food. When we had eaten, we spread blankets on the ground to sleep and huddled against one another like sheep in a barn. I heard the rolling of thunder. I was frightened. The night became chilly and we didn't have enough blankets.

It started to rain. I couldn't fall asleep. A drop of water seeped through the earthen ceiling and fell on my lips. I licked it. It tasted of earth and I spat it out. Then a second drop fell, and a third, and this went on without stopping. I called my mother. She got up and pushed me closer to my brother, put a plate to catch the raindrops where my lips had been, and went back to bed.

I stayed awake, listening to the tinkle of raindrops falling on the plate, and I curled into a tiny ball to get warm. My sister Ziné woke with a start from raindrops falling on her, but she went back to sleep right away. Between two raindrops, my mother got up, pushed my sister aside, and put down a second plate to collect rain. In a corner of the room we could hear other leaks. My mother got up and brought over a third plate. When drops fell on another of my sisters, our supply of plates was exhausted and my mother used a saucepan.

My father, whom I thought was asleep, pulled his tobacco pouch from under his pillow. Without opening his eyes, he rolled a cigarette for himself and started to smoke. I was delighted; there was someone else, like me, who wasn't sleeping. But his mind was on revenge. A raindrop fell on his chest yet he barely opened his eyes. On his blanket a moist stain slowly grew larger, but he didn't react. Then drops fell on his neck, on his forehead, but he went on smoking.

Only after five drops had fallen on his face and nine on his chest did he decide to get up. He took the oil lamp, went outside, and climbed up on the earthen roof to smooth it with the stone roller we used to fill up holes. In our room everything became wet. Just one small corner was still dry and the whole family took refuge there. We all glued our eyes to the ceiling.

My father's work on the roof had only made matters worse. He returned to the room with his shoes full of mud. He shook a foot to get rid of the earth and his shoe flew across the room. Then he came and collapsed next to us in his soaking clothes. We were all inert and silent. My mother got up and took a big pomegranate out of her bundle and divided it among us. It was a pomegranate from our orchard, and it sweetened our mouths.

I woke up. I was warm and dry. When I opened my eyes, my family was having breakfast and the spoons tinkled in the teacups. Sunbeams shone through the wide-open door and the little window, lighting up the room. I stretched out like a snake. Cheerful, I joined my family for breakfast. The silhouette of a man appeared at the door; he coughed to announce his presence and asked my father if he was ready. My father gulped down his glass of tea. He was already completely dressed, in his *sarwel** and the long black belt printed with small white tulips wound around his waist. He made sure his red-checked white turban was well adjusted on his head, then he turned to my mother and said, "I'm leaving." My mother answered, "OK."

My mother's face had lost its smile; she mourned her brother and the six other members of the family who had been killed.

But I was still a kid.

In front of the house, I saw little puddles left by the night storm. In the distance, the mountain and the chestnut groves

*Baggy trousers. —Translator's note

were bathed in a beautiful morning light. The blankets drying in the sun were the only unpleasant reminder of the night before. Curious, I walked around our house and approached a large cement building. I looked through the doorway and was astonished to see a huge woman, at least six feet tall, with straight blond hair, skin as white as cheese, and big blue eyes. She was dressed like a Kurd, the same as my mother, in a long, very colorful dress that fell to her ankles and a close-fitting vest. She smiled at me and asked if I was a child from the newly arrived family. Timid as a young calf, I nodded, yes. She called to her son to come play with me. I waited for this son with great curiosity, wondering what he would look like. He came out of the house and came toward me. I was disappointed: he was like me, dark eyes, black hair, olive skin. We were the same age. I looked at the mother and son and I wondered how such a woman could have produced a child like that; how this fair blond angel, this extraterrestrial being, could have given birth to this swarthy boy with a gypsy face like mine.

His name was Rezgar and we became good friends. We went to fetch water. I didn't know where the well was, but Rezgar told me we would go to the river, to the banks of the Zab. We meandered through the alleyways of the village, and had just passed the last house when I stopped. I couldn't believe my eyes. Before me was another woman as tall as Rezgar's mother, with the same hair color, skin, and blue eyes. She too dressed like a Kurd, but her clothes seemed to me even more beautiful than my mother's.

Rezgar had kept walking. I ran to catch up with him, and soon we reached the banks of the Zab. It was a wide river, with a strong current. The water was clear. On the other side, there were Iraqi soldiers. It was the frontier.

Billē was a tiny village compared to my town of Aqra, but here there was no government official and everything was under the control of General Barzani, the leader of the

Kurds. Ever since we had arrived, men had come to fetch my father, and he would disappear for several days with them. He was summoned by the general to intercept and decode Iraqi messages and send instructions in Morse code to our fighters. My father was General Barzani's Morse code operator. He often used to say to my mother, "Haybet, I'm the general's personal operator," smoothing his mustache between his thumb and his index finger.

We owned two partridges, a wardrobe, and an old Soviet radio that my father listened to all day long. And me, I went back to school, where the teaching was in Kurdish. For my father, my schooling was essential; he wanted me to become a judge or a lawyer. I learned our national anthem: "*Ey Raquib, her maye qeumé kurd ziman* . . . Oh my friends, be assured the Kurdish people are alive and nothing can bring down their flag . . ."

Thanks to my teacher, Abdul Rahman, and his magic violin, I learned other songs. He was the teacher, headmaster, and janitor of the school.

Abdul Rahman was a bachelor and he came from Erbil. We students helped him with the cleaning, and in the winter we brought him firewood and cleared the snow from the roof. When there was a good meal at home, we invited him. He was a simple and discreet man.

On a day when the sun was hot, I came home from school, put down my books, took off my clothes, and ran straight down to the river completely naked with Rezgar. Intoxicated by our race, we behaved like lunatics and jumped in the river. I felt living things lightly touching my skin. All my senses were alert. I popped my head out of the water, eyes wide open. Everything around me was brown and stirring. My head, my hair, my ears, my entire body was covered with wriggling worms: I was bathing in a river of worms. Panicked, I swam for the bank with my eyes closed and came out of the water waving my arms in every direction to get rid of the creatures. Suddenly I heard a big laugh: it was my mother. This was the first time I'd seen her smile since the day my cousin's body was dragged behind the jeep.

She looked at me but didn't come to help me, and went on laughing hysterically. It was April and in the spring worms wiggled up to the topsoil. When the snow thawed, little streams of water rose, loosening clumps of earth filled with worms and carrying them down to the river.

On the way home we passed another woman with blond hair and blue eyes, and I forgot about the worms. I turned to my mother and asked, "How many are there?"

"They're Russian," she said. She told me that in 1946, when the Kurdish Republic in Iran fell, our leader, Mustafa Barzani, who had been appointed general, had held out against the Iranians to the end, refusing to surrender. But the Iranian army, aided by the Turks and Iraqis, had broken his resistance. He and a few hundred men had no choice but to take refuge in the USSR. They stayed there for many years, and then came to Iraq when the royal family was deposed in 1958. Some of Barzani's partisans had married Russian women who had been widowed during the Second World War. And so the mystery was solved.

In early summer 1968, my father spent his days listening to Radio Baghdad. I couldn't understand Arabic at all, but I could sense that something was happening. In the village, all the men kept their weapons within reach. Two names kept being mentioned on the radio; I knew them by heart: Ahmed Hassan al-Bakr and Saddam Hussein al-Takriti, the two putsch leaders. Word went out that the government was going to attack us. Everyone waited for instructions from our leader, General Barzani. One word, one sign from him, and my father's Brno was ready to be fired. When the order came, he stood up immediately and grabbed the old Czech rifle. A horse was waiting for him. My father turned to my mother and said, "I'm leaving." My mother replied, "OK." I never heard her say any other word when he left.

Several days went by and nothing happened. Little by little, life returned to normal. As for my father, he came home on a new horse the general had given him, and he had a new Brno. He claimed that his rifle was so precise he could hit a cigarette butt from a distance of eleven hundred yards. He was very proud of his Brno and often said to my mother that with this kind of weapon, he could take on a thousand soldiers and Omar Akha's entire clan. It was the perfect gun with which to avenge the deaths of seven members of our family.

I realized that whenever my father was home, General Barzani was absent from his Raizan headquarters; he was visiting his fighters. He didn't need my father.

Having cleaned his new rifle, my father started listening to the radio again, moving around in the one room to get the best reception for the latest news. He was relieved; he heard that the new government did not intend to attack us. The radio even said that the two putsch leaders were not hostile to Kurds.

Yet one detail worried my father: the name of the new party—the Baath Party, the party of the Arab Socialist Resurrection.

We still couldn't go home to our town of Aqra. We were homesick for our town, our house, our relatives, our family graves. As for me, I missed my cousin Cheto and his stunt pigeons, the pomegranates from our orchard, and the bulb that lit up our evenings. When could we retrieve our memories? We believed our leader, General Barzani, when he told us that freedom was close at hand. But as we waited for freedom, a lot of time went by.

Late one night my father heard a noise behind the door. He pulled out his Brno from under the mattress, got up, and cocked the gun. All of us were awake. The door opened slowly. My father was in firing position, his finger on the trigger. A young man with a wisp of a mustache on his upper lip came through the door. It was Dilovan, my eighteen-year-old brother. The rifle fell from my father's hands and he threw himself into his son's arms, overcome with joy. My mother and the rest of us followed suit. We were all crying tears of happiness. We hadn't seen him in three years.

We turned up the flame in the oil lamp, and we all sat around him. My mother sought her son's odor on his neck. He took off his jacket; she took it and raised it to her face. If my father hadn't reminded her, she would have forgotten to prepare tea.

When she returned with the tea, she picked up my brother's jacket again and placed it on her knees. We devoured my brother with our eyes, drank in his every word. He told us about his life as a *peshmerga*. Like my father, he was convinced that after one more year of struggle and sacrifice we would obtain independence. A sweet thrill ran through our bodies. One more year, and Kurdistan would be ours.

My mother held up the oil lamp near her son to see him better, but my father pushed the lamp away; he didn't want his son bothered by the smoke. And my mother kept sniffing his jacket and saying, "It's my son's odor." Later that night, in a tender voice, she said, "My son, you're a man now, you're eighteen, you must marry . . . We want to see our grandson." My brother was embarrassed. He was an adolescent; he didn't speak of women in front of his parents. He smiled vaguely and said only, "It's up to you."

As for me, I was very happy. Like my mother, I couldn't take my eyes off him. It is marvelous to have a big brother.

Before dawn, I put my head on my mother's knees, eyes still riveted on Dilovan, and fell asleep like the kid I was.

One evening in July, my father was listening to Radio Baghdad, Voice of the People, and simultaneously translating everything into Kurdish for us. The announcer from the Baath Party, the new pan-Arab party, was inviting all Iraqis in Baghdad to come eat kebab in Liberation Square, in front of the gallows where enemies of the people and the homeland had been hanged. He shouted, "Oh, Iraqi people, from now on we shall liberate your country from its enemies." The hanged men were Baghdadis: Iraqis and Iraqi Jews.

On hearing that Jews were being hanged in Baghdad, my father became frightened in Billē, miles from Baghdad . . .

His father, my grandfather Selim Malay Shero, had taken Aïcha the Jewish woman as his second wife. Aïcha's family had moved to Israel before I was born, but she had stayed in Aqra. She loved my grandfather and even after his death never wanted to leave the country; she wanted to be near his grave. Everyone in our town knew about this and knew my grandfather had been madly in love with Aïcha the Jewish woman. People even said that he would have followed her to Israel. And that one day while his entire harvest was burning, my grandfather was in bed with Aïcha, refusing to move, not wanting to shatter their bliss.

I saw fear on my father's face. He saw himself among the hanged men in Liberation Square, surrounded by crowds eating kebab, because his father had been in love with Aïcha the Jewish woman, his stepmother.

I left my father to his thoughts and ran after my brother Dilovan. He took me to visit the few shops in the village. I looked around for some trinket he might buy me. The first store sold only kilims; in the back, a Brno was hanging on a wall. There was nothing there for me. The second store sold riding accessories, and horsemen were assembled in front of the door with their mounts. The next store had farming tools. Finally, in a stall a bit farther on, among dusty oil cans and sacks of sugar and tea, I noticed packages of biscuits in a corner. We looked at each other, my brother and I, and then went in. All the merchandise had been smuggled in from Iran, for Baghdad had imposed an embargo on the regions controlled by our leader, Barzani.

My brother picked up a package of biscuits and my mouth watered. They were honey and sesame biscuits. I could already feel them melting in my mouth. I kept my eye on the package while my brother turned it over this way and that. I was waiting for a sign from him to grab it. After what seemed to me an eternity, he handed the biscuits back to the salesman and told me to follow him. We walked out. I was terribly disappointed; my mouth was dry and I had a lump in my throat. He turned to me. "Azad," he said, "those are good biscuits, but the ones in that package had more bugs in them than sesame. Come on, I'll buy you something else." I knew there was no other store for me in Billē. The last shop was the meeting place of partridge enthusiasts; the partridge is a common bird in our mountains and a symbol of our people. I knew the partridge could be its own worst enemy: hunters used the birds as bait to attract their fellow creatures. But I didn't understand why my mother sometimes compared us Kurds to partridges, for I was still a kid.

We arrived at Hamadouk's tearoom. We climbed the ladder up to the balcony, the ground floor being reserved for the barber. It was a modest tearoom with small, rickety stools and dented drums as tables. A large sign said CASINO, but there was nothing to drink but tea. The customers around us were playing dominoes, their guns resting on their laps. My brother raised his hand to greet them; we sat down and he ordered tea.

I didn't want any, but there wasn't anything else for me. Then Dilovan sent me downstairs to the barber to get my hair cut. I had a choice between several cuts and I chose the one where a bowl is placed on top of your head and the barber cuts your hair all around the edge. I ended up looking like my Billē schoolmates, with a skullcap of hair on my head. I was sure I would be the only boy with this haircut in all of Aqra.

After that we went home. My father was a bit worried. He whispered to my brother. Dilovan had to go back to the mountains, urgently. At my mother's insistence, he ate some *savar** and a few olives before leaving. It was always painful to see my brother go. My mother cried. But it was clear that the situation was deteriorating.

On my father's radio set, Radio Moscow denounced the two putsch leaders and presented General Barzani as the liberator of the Kurdish people. But Voice of America said the Kurds were rebels and bandits, and Radio Baghdad continued to accuse us—our leader and all of us—of being Zionist agents and enemies of the Baath Party. The two putsch leaders spoke of going after other enemies once they had crushed the Jews.

The Iraqi army began to bomb some of our villages. There was turmoil all around us once again: horses and mules crossed through the village, loaded with weapons.

Hamadouk's "Casino" was crowded with *peshmergas*. They drank a beverage served in bottles. It wasn't tea; the color was darker. After drinking it, they belched loudly. I was very

*Cracked wheat. —Translator's note

curious to know what it was and how it tasted, but I didn't have the money to buy a bottle of the mysterious drink. I watched Hamadouk's gestures, perplexed. He opened the bottle with a piece of metal; it made a strange noise, like a bullet fired into water. As soon as the black bottle was open, a white foam bubbled out of it. Rezgar and I immediately started collecting the bottle caps and soon our pockets were filled with them. When I was alone, I quietly sniffed a recently removed cap and licked it with the tip of my tongue. It was impossible to tell what that strange drink tasted of.

Suddenly two airplanes flew overhead at a low altitude. Panic broke out; some people hid, others lay on the ground. I remained standing, petrified, my heart about to burst, when Rajab jumped down from the balcony, threw himself on me, and shoved me against the wall. Aiming his old rifle up at the sky, he started shooting at the airplanes. I smelled the odor of gunpowder, and the airplanes flew off. Rajab proudly slung his gun over his shoulder and got ready to climb back up on the balcony. He caressed my hair. "You weren't scared, were you?" he asked. I'd been terrified, but I shook my head, for Kurds must not be scared. Then he added, "Whose son are you?" "I'm Shero's son." His face lit up. "Oh yes, you're Shero's son—Shero, the general's operator." "Yes," I said. Then he looked up at Hamadouk, the "Casino" owner, who was just coming out of his hiding place behind the samovar, and called to him, "Bring a bottle for this future *peshmerga*." He turned to me and asked, "What's your name?" "Azad." "A beautiful name . . ."

Hamadouk brought us two bottles, one black, the other yellow. "Which one do you want?" asked Rajab. Shyly I answered, "I don't want anything." But Rajab insisted, pointing to the bottles. "See, the black one is Coke; the yellow one's Orangina. It's good, you can drink some." I refused again, shaking my head. Rajab turned away from me and started climbing up the ladder, saying to Hamadouk, "His

name is Azad, he's Shero's son, the general's personal operator." I watched him with a lump in my throat. I was dying to
taste one of the drinks but I was afraid my mother would be
angry. Out of pride, she forbade us to accept anything from
strangers. Before leaving us, Rajab called down to me from
the balcony, "Tell your father that Rajab sends his greetings."
I nodded my head, and I left with a heavy heart from not
having drunk from the mysterious bottle.

My cousin Gibrail, Mamou's brother, came to see us. We
hadn't seen him in a long time. During lunch, we were talking about Mamou, with tears in our eyes, when we heard
the sound of airplanes. They were flying very low, making
the tea glasses shake. We rushed out of the house to hide,
fearing the house might collapse on our heads. No bomb
was dropped, but the dreadful sound of the low-flying planes
was enough to make me think I would die of fear. The
planes came around again, even more menacingly. We all
dived to the ground, facedown, and the pane in our one
window shattered into pieces. Our horse, tied up, kicked
and whinnied in fear, and the partridges, terror-stricken,
desperately tried to break open the bars of their cage with
their beaks. Calm returned; Gibrail kissed us and left hur-
riedly for Raizan, worried about his two wives and sixteen
children. From that day on, the planes flew overhead regularly. Nothing was more terrifying to me than that noise.
One day, they started to bomb our village. Hidden, I saw my
father fire with his Brno in the direction of the planes. But
what could he do with a Czech rifle dating from the 1940s?

Henceforth, at dawn the entire village went to hide in the
caves along the river, and so did we. We brought along the
little food we had and stayed hidden all day in our caves.
We didn't leave until sunset, taking the same road back for
the two miles that separated us from our house.

It wasn't long before we had nothing left to eat but flat

round breads soaked in tea, and then only once a day. All activities came to a halt. When a bread crumb fell to the ground, out of respect I would pick it up, kiss it, and bring it to my forehead before eating it. Bread is sacred. In full view, the river Zab flowed by, a river full of rocks and whirlpools, teeming with fish. Our cave was a short distance away.

My father knew that in other caves the villagers fished, but he said nothing. We knew it, too, but we kept silent; we didn't want to humiliate my father; he didn't know how to swim. How can you fish if you don't know how to swim?

With our ever more stringent diet, we all began to get thin. It was unbearable for my father, seeing his family die of hunger, so he decided to go fishing no matter what. The limpid water flowed by; the fish in the river taunted us, leaping and lively; we devoured them with our eyes. My father made himself a fishing rod with a branch, a piece of string, a needle bent like a hook, and some bread as bait. Perched on a large flat stone and surrounded by his whole family, he threw his line into the water, but he didn't catch a single fish. By the end of the day, an entire loaf of bread had vanished in the river to feed the fish. "It's because of the airplanes, the fish don't dare approach," was the excuse my father came up with, even though we could see the fish, right there under our noses. A second day went by, just like the first. As soon as the airplanes disappeared, we came out of the cave to encourage my father, still on the rock. We saw the smoke rising from grills in the neighboring caves and the smell of grilled fish tortured our stomachs.

My father felt more and more ashamed, and my mother moistened the dry bread and divided the pieces among us. My father broke his bread into six pieces and gave each of us a piece, claiming he had a stomachache and would just drink a cup of tea and smoke a cigarette. After this meal, he started fishing again, with his line a few yards away from his feet. "Cast it farther out," said my mother. "Very good, but if the hook gets caught in the rocks, who'll go fetch it?" "Me," I said, raising my head. He looked at me, surprised: he didn't know I had learned to swim with my pal Rezgar. He wanted me to demonstrate my swimming skills at the edge of the river. I undressed and threw myself into the stream, stark naked. "Come back!" cried my father. It was dangerous, but I was cocksure.

Then I heard them all scream. The world collapsed around us; the planes were bombing the river with napalm, and huge columns of water soared up into the sky wherever the bombs fell. I started swimming like a maniac toward the riverbank, where I could see my whole family, looking panicked, reaching out their arms to me. My father unwound his long belt, put one end in my mother's hand, threw the other out to me, and jumped into the water. The bombs went on falling and I came out without his help. My mother, tugging on the belt, now tried to pull my father to the riverbank, but the powerful current made it hard. We all set about helping her, hauling our father out of the water like a big dead fish. We looked at him standing on the riverbank, dripping wet. In tears, we burst out laughing and retreated to our cave.

Before long we heard only the sound of the river, so my father went out to look at the sky and dry himself off in the sun. Moments later he came back, completely naked, his arms loaded with fish, which he threw down on the ground. Incredulous, we rushed to look at them. They were all mangled. We could easily imagine that we had been within a hairsbreadth of suffering the same fate as the fish. "Fix them, Haybet," said my father, turning to go out. My father's thin silhouette was outlined against the light at the entrance to the cave. This was the first time I'd seen my father naked.

We set about preparing the fish. We all realized that if we wanted to eat, the airplanes would have to return every day.

My father always kept telling us, "In a year, our country will be liberated." And the years went by. Then we began to believe it. The two putsch leaders in Baghdad, al–Bakr and Saddam, spoke of peace, and the planes stopped coming. My brother Dilovan returned from the hills. My mother had found him a wife—Dijla, Barakat's daughter. My brother had never set eyes on Dijla. Barakat had agreed to the marriage on one condition: that we give our sister Taman to his son Goran. My sister had never set eyes on Goran. This was of no consequence—my mother had seen all four, and the marriages were celebrated.

My parents were proud of their new daughter-in-law. She had an uncle who had followed General Barzani to the Soviet Union in 1946, and that was enough for them. My parents gave the young bride a gift of gold earrings. My mother had a small jewelry case in which she hoarded our entire treasure: several rings, necklaces, a solid gold bracelet, and a cake of soap, the last one purchased in our town of Aqra. It was a deluxe soap called Asfanik. Dijla, our young sister-in-law, couldn't pronounce Asfanik; she'd say Afsanik. Whenever she annoyed us, my little sister and me, we'd tease her by asking, "What soap is it?" She'd mispronounce it and we'd make fun of her, the village girl. But Dijla had a great deal of personality. She was intelligent, even though she didn't know how to read and write, which very much bothered my brother. The day after their marriage, my brother came home with some paper and a pencil. He closeted himself with his wife in the one room of our house and taught her the alphabet. Alphabet or no, we had to stay outside; the young married couple was not to be disturbed. When he left for the mountains again, he gave her a pile of homework as an assignment, and that was how my sister-in-law learned to read. And we children, we thought about our sister Taman, whom we had exchanged for Dijla: she knew how to read and write.

After his marriage, my older brother returned home often. We'd go to the village with him; we'd listen to cassettes of Kurdish songs in Hamadouk's "Casino," where the ambiance was very lively. I no longer craved the parasite-infested Iranian biscuits; I was determined to get someone to buy me a bottle of the black liquid. When Hamadouk asked me what I wanted, I answered without hesitation, "Some Coke," and my brother Rostam followed suit. Rajab, that proud and courageous man, was there. He was talking to my brother Dilovan. Rostam and I, we took advantage of the opportunity to order two bottles of Orangina. Suddenly Hamadouk turned off the music to listen to the news. All the men gathered around the radio. There was an announcement that General Barzani had been invited to Baghdad. And my brother and I emptied our bottles; then, mouths agape, we belched at length. Around us, the spirited conversations went on. Rajab said that the general shouldn't go to Baghdad, and he got all worked up. "If they're sincere, let the putsch leaders come to us! Why should the general trust them?" They all took bets: would he or would he not go to Baghdad? The stakes were bottles of Coke and Orangina. Some of the men even bet their horses or their best partridges. Rajab went so far as to bet his Brno that the general wouldn't go. And he won. It was Saddam who ended up traveling to the mountains. Except for the independence of Kurdistan, he accepted all the demands. Kurds and Arabs, we were going to share everything like brothers!

From then on, everyone had a smile on their lips. We were all carried away by the euphoria of peace. I certainly believed in it: the price of Coke went down, I could buy myself two and a half bottles of Coke for the price of one, and in joyful celebration, my father fired into the sky with his Brno. There was dancing in the streets of Billē, accompanied by drums and flutes. Even my mother, tiny among the tall Russian women, danced with joy, arms raised in the air. We were finally a free people. My father sold his two horses. We gathered our possessions. An old pickup truck came to fetch us. After I had embraced Rezgar and his mother, the towering Russian lady, and everyone in the village, I saw my teacher, Abdul Rahman, arrive, holding a scroll of paper. He embraced us and handed me the scroll: it was my school certificate. The entire family piled into the truck, with us children perched on bundles in the rear. My father entrusted the partridge cage to me and slipped his Brno under a mattress, muttering between his teeth, "You never know . . ." He climbed in front with my mother, and we set off to go back home to Aqra. We waved our hands, *Khatra wa, khatra wa*★ . . . We were leaving my sister Taman behind but taking Dijla with us.

On arriving in Aqra, the truck stopped about a hundred yards from our house. My mother rushed toward it first, like a madwoman. All our relatives and friends came out to greet us, but nothing and no one could stop our racing forward. The whole neighborhood started running with us, kissing us, welcoming us. Suddenly, when she got to our house, my mother stopped, transfixed. All that was left were a few sections of blackened wall. She made her way into the rubble in tears. She caressed the walls with her hands as she might have caressed the mortal remains of a loved one.

She wept. We all started weeping with her, and the

★Goodbye. —Translator's note

neighbors with us. After meticulously inspecting what remained of our house, she went into the garden. It was overrun with grass and the dried stalks of flowers. And in the orchard of pomegranate trees, fig trees, olive trees, cherry trees, apricot trees, and grapevines, only the trunks were left. She stopped at every decapitated tree and she wept, and everyone wept along with her. I couldn't bear it anymore. I went back to the ruins of our house. I saw my father, alone, squatting, a cigarette between his fingers, and I heard him sobbing.

We all met again in the garden, and tongues loosened. No, our sacrifice had not been in vain; we were free. Faces brightened and the time came for joy. I left my family as soon as I caught sight of Cheto, my cousin with the stunt pigeons. He was standing off to one side, looking at me; he was waiting for me. Happily, I went up to him. We looked at each other and stood side by side to see who was bigger: he was a little taller than I. And then we went off to fly some pigeons.

I spent the summer of our return to Aqra joyfully carrying sandbags. My father had received financial compensation to rebuild our house. He called on Housta Musto, the best builder in town. Musto began by inspecting the ruins of the old house, then he drew a blueprint: four bedrooms, a spacious living room, for there was plenty of land. My father carefully studied Musto's blueprint while smoking a cigarette. He shook his head; he wasn't pleased. "No, Musto, no, it's too big, too exposed, there are too many windows!" Musto, surprised, defended his blueprint. After lengthy discussions, he came up with another plan: a beautiful villa with large openings giving out on our orchard. Again, my father wasn't pleased. In the end, Musto gave up. "Fine," he said to my father, "do your own plan, and I'll carry it out," and he left, disappointed. He couldn't understand what my father wanted.

My father had known nothing but war. He was obsessed with problems of safety. He spent the night thinking about his house plan, and in the morning he sent me to fetch Musto. Musto didn't challenge the plan which my father drew for him on the ground with a stick: two rooms on the ground floor, two on the next floor, all the windows oriented away from the town, facing the orchard and the hills. Poor Musto listened to my father's explanations with some misgivings. But my father, imperturbable, continued, "A wall one yard thick, built of stone and cement. That's much more resistant than the paper-thin sheets you're proposing." Then, stabbing the ground with his stick, "There are too many openings in your plan. Some of the windows have to be eliminated. We must be protected from bullets no matter what angle they fire on us from. You didn't anticipate this in your blueprint. And think of the walls; I want walls that can hold up to missiles." Musto, losing patience, grabbed the stick from my father. "Do you want to build a fortress or a house?" "A fortress-house, Musto, a fortress-house," my father replied. So then Musto spoke to him as to a child. "Shero dear, the war is over. We're free and there's peace now. Why are you always thinking of war? The time has come to build large, airy, welcoming houses." Scratching his bald head under his turban, my father had the last word: "That's true, Musto. But the saying is the bride must please her husband, and you, you must build a house that pleases me." Musto didn't want to lose the job.

By the time the first stone was laid, I had already brought over a big pile of sand.

When the house was finished, my father hung a large portrait of General Barzani in the main room. Outside, the orchard had been cleared, the dead trees uprooted, and the garden was once again overflowing with flowers.

I was in eighth grade. Cheto was three grades ahead of me, and Ramo, another cousin, one grade below. We were all in the same school. Over the door, a banner proclaimed, "Long Live Arab-Kurd Friendship."

I was a good student; I loved school. My father was constantly telling me that he wanted me to become a judge or a lawyer. But on the first day of school I couldn't understand a word: the teacher spoke Arabic. I was shattered. My enthusiasm vanished. I was on the verge of tears. I felt self-conscious with my classmates; I was nothing but an incompetent, an ass. Cheto and Ramo waited for me after school. I didn't stop and didn't talk to them and went straight home. My mother saw me crying and she wanted to know why. Tearfully, I explained my distress. "I didn't understand anything the teacher was saying; he speaks only Arabic." My mother caressed my head, smiling. "Dear boy, a class in Arabic is nothing to worry about; it's good to learn another language." I answered, annoyed, "But, Mama, it isn't just one class. Everything is in Arabic." Whereupon my father arrived. "Don't worry, my son, before the end of the year the teaching will be in Kurdish; the government promised us. You'll be first in your class."

The teacher never called on me, I was never punished, and every day I made the same wish—that the courses in Kurdish would begin. In vain. I was forced to learn Arabic. As the end of the year approached, it was exam time, and still no change. Everything continued in Arabic. I waited for the results, hoping that my teacher would be lenient and I would pass into the higher grade. When the day came, all the students lined up in the courtyard. The headmaster, report cards in hand, called us up one by one. We knew we had passed when the teacher signaled us to go up to the caretaker. By custom, the student first gave the caretaker a coin to thank him for his services in the past year. Then, when the student received his report card, we were supposed to applaud. My father had given me a one-dirham coin for the caretaker. I held it carefully in my hand, buried deep inside my pocket, and fiddled with it as I waited to be called. Suddenly I heard my name, my head began to spin, and I became unaware of my surroundings. I headed for the caretaker automatically and put my coin in his box without waiting for my teacher's signal. There was a great silence. The headmaster signaled the caretaker to hand my dirham back to me.

I still didn't realize that the worst had happened, and I went on waiting for my teacher's lips to pronounce the much awaited word: "passed." All the students were looking at me. Without a word, the headmaster gave me my report card. I took it, eyes lowered, and heard the next name being called, "Cheto Rasul." I walked away under the ripple of applause for my cousin.

I looked at my report card and saw the red marks; I had been flunked. I thought of not going home, fearing my parents' reaction.

My father greeted me very calmly and all he said was, "My son, my dream is that you become a judge or a lawyer. Your older brother, Dilovan, didn't go to university; he joined the fighters. And Rostam didn't even finish high school. I must have one son at least who will allow me to walk with my head high." He was sad, disappointed, and after a minute of silence he smacked me in the face. He didn't speak to me for several days. Ramo had caught up with me. Small comfort. We'd be in the same class in the fall, and I hoped our teacher would let us share the same bench.

My father was summoned to the town hall. He went hoping to get a job, by virtue of the agreements concluded between General Barzani and the Iraqi government.* The government employee told him he had been put on early retirement and would be receiving a small pension. For my father, this was a bad omen.

*In March 1970 the Kurds obtained an agreement that accorded them partial autonomy and allowed Barzani to keep 15,000 armed Kurdish troops.

On the other hand, the teacher-training course my brother Dilovan had taken in the mountains was accredited by the state, and he found a job in a small village far away. He spent a good part of his salary paying for visits to his wife, who, with their little daughter, was living at our house. They had named her Zilan, after a valley where the Turks exterminated Kurdish deportees in the 1930s, to mark their commitment to the cause.

Xebat (The Struggle), the Kurds' underground newspaper, became legal and we could now buy it openly. One day, my father came home with the newspaper and a thick book tucked under his arm. It was Malaye Djeziri's poems. What a marvelous book! Each poem was illustrated by a painting. From then on, late at night, after he had listened to the news on all the stations, Radio Baghdad, Radio Israel, Radio Moscow, and Voice of America, my father would open the thick book and read us poems, written in very beautiful Kurdish. He would comment on them for us, giving free rein to his imagination. But what fascinated me were the magnificent illustrations facing the poems. This was the first time I had seen drawings and I was overwhelmed to discover this magical art. I thought that since these drawings were so beautiful, the poetry must be very beautiful, too.

They showed magnificent women, voluptuous like the houris of paradise, springing up from the earth like flowers. The sky was as limpid as the sky in our mountains. These beautiful women were dressed as Kurds. I longed to touch them, to speak to them. I would have liked to hang them on the wall next to the general's portrait. For me, being Kurdish meant these poems and the songs I had learned, these women in long green or pomegranate-colored jackets embroidered with small violet flowers.

At first, I thought the poems were little songs without music. Thanks to the drawings, I realized that if the poetry gave rise to such beauty, it undoubtedly surpassed simple song lyrics. And with this book, published openly, I thought we Kurds were beginning to gain respect.

Some time later, walking by Abdulla's barbershop—Abdulla, whom people called a Communist—I saw a large painting and stopped. It was a painting from my father's poetry book titled *The Young Kurdish Girl* and signed "Sami." While my friend Ramo, suddenly sick to his stomach, rushed to the toilet in the mosque to empty himself of all the pomegranates and figs he had gorged on, I lingered in front of the barbershop, transfixed, eyes riveted on the painting.

From then on, I went by the shop whenever I could. One day, I saw my brother Dilovan inside, and he called out to me immediately. The shop was the meeting place of all the town intellectuals. My brother was talking with a very tastefully dressed young man. His name was Sami, and they were discussing the painting. My brother pushed me toward one of the chairs and asked the barber to cut my hair while they continued talking.

There was no question, I was close to Sami, creator of the painting. I wanted to touch him or kiss his hand or talk to him, yet at the same time I wanted to run away. I was greatly intimidated. Abdulla wrapped a large, well-worn towel around me and tilted the chair back.

I would gladly have stayed in that chair for hours because I could see Sami in the mirror. Alas, Abdulla cut my hair in the blink of an eye and that was it; my brother said goodbye to Sami and we left.

I fell ill. I had persistent bouts of high fever. In spite of this, my mother took my hand and walked with me to a desolate hill facing our house. Near the top, at the opening of a cave, we stopped. It was a sacred cave.

Inside was a spring flowing with cool, clear water and

surrounded by twigs on which pieces of green and pink fabric had been fastened. My mother undressed me and, with a saucer, poured sacred water all over me. This cave was called *Kinishte*, the synagogue. It had been a Jewish place of worship for a very long time. Until the 1950s, there had been a Jewish quarter in our town and two synagogues, besides the three churches and the mosque. Then the Jews had left for Israel and the mosques had multiplied. Legend had it that a holy Jewish man was buried in the cave. This mattered little to my mother; a holy man was a holy man, whether Jewish, Christian, or Muslim.

Coming out of the cave, we passed some Iraqi soldiers. They were building blockhouses. I saw the alarm on my mother's face, but I didn't attach too much importance to it. I was still a kid.

A year went by and I passed my exams, to my father's great satisfaction. With his ear glued to the radio, he was following the putsch leader Saddam Hussein's trip to Moscow. And to his great disappointment, Radio Moscow made no mention of the Kurds. I went to town to look at Sami's paintings. Many shops showed his paintings now. Sami wasn't just painting young Kurdish girls anymore. One of his paintings showed four partridges on a snowy mountaintop, symbolizing our homeland split up among four countries. One of my favorites was a portrait of the charismatic General Barzani, head held high, in traditional dress, a dagger tucked in his belt, a pistol at his left side, the end of his rifle jutting out behind his shoulder. What a great man. A rumor had been going around for some time that the general wasn't coming down from his mountains anymore. He no longer believed that the accords signed with the putsch leaders would be respected. We had seen policemen gradually reappear in town. That was not in the accords. And on the hill with the cave, directly facing our house, the Iraqi soldiers' little block-houses had been converted into barracks. I knew that had it been possible, my father would have turned his house around to face the town.

My cousin Cheto used to sell blackberries to the soldiers, and I would go with him. We sold them for ten cents a cup. We never went farther than the barracks door. At first, the soldiers distrusted us. They would ask us to eat some of the berries in their presence so they could be sure they weren't poisoned. The trade became unprofitable: we had to eat a cup of blackberries for every few cups we sold. But little by little, they began to trust us, and the soldiers going on leave to their families asked us for whole baskets of apricots, apples, grapes, figs . . .

It was marvelous; we were beginning to earn money and I was building a small nest egg. My mother, though, was afraid for us because of the soldiers and the land mines in the area. With money from the blackberries I went to see Sami in his newly opened studio, where he also sold tubes of paint. He taught me how to stretch canvas on a frame. When I came back home, I climbed up to the second floor with a white canvas and the fat book of poetry by Malaye Djeziri under my arm. I studied every illustration in the book over and over again, inch by inch. I read through the poems, trying to understand which words had inspired the colors, the shape of a mouth, the black eyes with long lashes, the hair, or the round breast, plump as the pomegranates in our orchard. Yes, there were even bare-breasted girls. I remained indecisive in front of my white canvas for the longest time, unable to pick up the paintbrushes. Suddenly I heard my brother Rostam arrive and I went downstairs to the garden.

He had a new weapon and was examining it with my

father. It was a Plimout. The weapon was the size of his forearm, unlike my father's long Brno. Besides, it was an automatic, and the magazine held thirty-six bullets. It was a short-range combat weapon. I was fascinated. My father placed the Plimout in my hands. "Be careful, it's loaded. With the slightest jolt, a hail of bullets can go off." I was dying to shoot a little, and my father added, "You're not a kid anymore, you're a man. Take it and fire as many bullets as you like." For the first time, thanks to the Plimout, my father called me a man. I seized the weapon and I darted off, running through the orchard toward the hills. I was proud— I had a weapon and I wasn't a kid anymore. I felt like a man, as my father had said. I looked all around me for a target. There was a flock of birds, but they were flying too high in the sky. I tried to find a rabbit or a snake, but no luck. Finally I aimed my weapon up at the sky, in the direction of God, and I fired a hail of bullets. I was like a madman, a drunk. At that moment, I could have killed a man, I was fearless. I fired a few more rounds and listened to the hail of bullets echo in the hills. The odor of gunpowder was intoxicating. Virile. After emptying the magazine of its thirty-six bullets, I smelled the barrel of the Plimout and headed back home, replete.

My mother killed a rooster and prepared a feast. My uncle Avdal Khan, who worked for the oil company, had just been put on early retirement. The government no longer wanted Kurds in sensitive positions, such as in the oil sector. And my uncle had decided to return to his hometown.

I was delighted. I had new pals—my cousin Sardar and especially his sister Shahla. She and I were the same age and she was very beautiful.

But the most beautiful thing was that my uncle came back with a television set! A television!

In the evening, as soon as the programs were to begin, I darted over to their house. First we had the privilege of hearing the party anthem, followed by endless speeches by President al-Bakr and Vice President Saddam Hussein. I was seeing the two Baath leaders for the first time. I looked at them, incredulous. Al-Bakr was an old man; he looked like our neighbor Babik the ice-cream vendor. But Saddam was young and slender, with a black mustache, and he was taken seriously because he very seldom smiled. Soon I could no longer bear to sit through the anthems or the speeches to the glory of Pan-Arabism and Baath nationalism. I would come in time for the Egyptian soap opera *Anter and Abla*. The plot revolved around a wealthy young man, Anter, who was in love with Abla, a black slave. The entire neighborhood talked about my uncle Avdal Khan's television. We all wanted one, except my mother, who regarded TV as the devil.

When my father received his meager pension, he added to it a little money he had saved and bought a television set. I went with him. It was a small set that worked on a car battery. The owner switched the set on. We saw the image of Saddam Hussein appear, bright and clear, and he quickly switched off the set. My father stood up, and after protracted bargaining, the deal was settled. The understanding was that once the set was bought, it couldn't be returned. We went home. My father was pleased with his purchase and I was delighted. The television was set up in the upstairs bedroom. To please my father more, my mother fixed us some good tea. The entire family sat down in front of the set while my father tried to tune in the image. But it remained blurry, the tea got cold, and we began to lose all hope of seeing *Anter and Abla*, our favorite soap opera. My mother asked my father, "Why did you buy a television set that runs with a battery when we have electricity?" My father didn't answer. He started to get worked up, turning the antenna in every direction. Our enthusiasm vanished, and worriedly we watched our father seething. We knew he was capable of anything in this state.

My father began to realize he had been swindled, and for the benefit of the salesman, he screamed, "May my donkey bugger your wife!" Exasperated, he stopped to drink his glass of tea, which, having been poured long before, was cold by then. He became annoyed at my mother and threw the half-full glass against the wall. Fearing the worst, we all got up and went downstairs to the first floor to sleep. My mother muttered that he had let the devil into the house.

A little while later my father called to us: the image was in focus; we could come back. We got out of our beds and went upstairs, only to discover indistinct shadows that strained the eyes. Soon even the shadows disappeared. We went back to bed while my father continued to curse the salesman and his wife. At around two in the morning, my father got dressed to go out. All of us were awake, fearing he would take his Brno with him. Fortunately, he didn't. Holding the television under his arm, he told me to follow him. We went back to the salesman and made him get out of bed. He understood as soon as he saw us. He said only, "Couldn't you wait until morning?" My father cut him off with a dry, categorical "No." "Here's your TV, give me my money back." Seeing my father so furious, the man didn't argue, and we left.

There was still my uncle's television, but he was growing weary of the constant visits from the neighbors' children. At first, he had welcomed us with tea and fruits. We would settle down like little pashas in front of the Egyptian soap opera. Now, we had to ring the bell at least ten times before he'd open the door. I would sometimes ask my mother to come with me, so when he asked, "Who is it?" I could answer, "My mother and I." And I'd often ask my mother to answer instead of me. As soon as I was in front of the television, I'd make myself as inconspicuous as possible, huddling in a corner. I waited for the adults to go to bed before making myself comfortable.

After *Anter and Abla*, they ran a documentary about the fish in the sea narrated by a tall, thin, very serious man in a red hat who spoke for at least half an hour in a strange language that frightened me. I was well aware that we spoke Kurdish, that Iraqis spoke Arabic, and that the rest of the world spoke English. What mysterious language could the man possibly be speaking? My uncle's television also broadcast Indian films. But I was disappointed, for there was nothing in my language. I was very intrigued. Perhaps our voices couldn't be transmitted on a screen? Or perhaps the television language was chosen in the country where the sets were manufactured? I longed to watch Kurdish television. I knew that the most important thing for my father was that I become a judge or a lawyer, but my wish was to create a television that would speak our language. I saw myself simultaneously as an inventor, as a maker of shows like *Anter and Abla*, as a musician and singer. And I vowed that one day I would make that machine speak Kurdish.

In those days of peace, my town, Aqra, was bursting with life. Singers came from everywhere to give concerts, theater troupes performed epics and plays, including *Mem and Zim*, our *Romeo and Juliet*. I went to the shows in the school hall, surrounded by women and children, and we danced to Kurdish folk tunes.

This was the first time I saw young girls sing and dance on a public stage. Between each number, a master of ceremonies chanted proverbs about the glory of women, exhorting them to take part in the political and social struggle. "Women are half of our society," he said. "A lion is always a lion, whether male or female. You can't applaud with just one hand . . . A bird can't fly with just one wing . . ."

And we were all supposed to applaud.

Salma was one of the young girls appearing onstage. She

wore a yellow jacket, the color of General Barzani's party, dotted with red flowers. She was self-confident, and my brother was in love. He never missed any of her performances. I had no idea whether she was in love with him, but what counted was that my brother was in love with her.

My brother confided in my sisters. They spoke to my mother, who broached the subject with my father. Not a moment was wasted; my parents, along with several notables, went to request Salma's hand. Her family accepted. Wasn't Rostam the son of Shero, the general's personal operator? Rostam's wedding was celebrated with a concert of honking horns, hails of bullets from his Plimout, and shots fired from my father's old Brno. Who said weapons were meant only for warfare? From that day on, I never again saw my young sister-in-law onstage. Though a bird can't fly with just one wing, let others provide the wing—not my sister-in-law.

One day, my father came home agitated. He filled his tobacco pouch, pulled out his Brno from under the mattress, and went back to the party headquarters, followed by my brother, his Plimout in hand. The worst had just been avoided! A delegation of religious Iraqis had gone up to the mountains to meet with our general and to give him a golden Koran as a gift; without their knowledge, it had been filled with TNT by Saddam Hussein's agents. Just as they were presenting the Koran to the general, it exploded, but miraculously he escaped unharmed, protected by the man who was serving him tea. Order was later restored.* My father put his Brno away under the mattress and my brother's Plimout found its niche again above the conjugal bed. As for me, I filled baskets with figs and, against my mother's advice,

*This assassination attempt occurred in March 1974. —Translator's note

went to sell them to the soldiers in the barracks to earn some pocket money.

One Thursday, Cheto and I were standing behind the barbed wire of the barracks, crying out, "Figs, apricots, blackberries," when two soldiers walked toward us. They were not the young conscripts we were used to having as customers. They were older, stronger, and much tougher-looking. They were carrying truncheons and wearing the red armbands of the military police. We wanted to turn on our heels, but they called to us, "Children, don't leave. Bring us your fruit." As soon as we were near them, they pounced on us. They insulted us as they hit us. "Children of savages . . . You come here with your shitty fruit to spy on us!" They hit harder and harder, pummeling and kicking us. We were raw from their blows. Our fruit was trampled underfoot. When they had had enough, they let us run away, limping and stumbling, and shouted after us, "If you come back here, we'll cut off your heads like sheep."

When I returned to our neighborhood, I passed tearful women from our family, walking behind a coffin carried by the men, my father and my uncle in the lead. I went up to Ramo. "Who died?" "No one." "So what's this coffin for?" "It's empty." "Then why are the women crying?" "We're going to kill cousin Mushir." I asked why, but he made no reply.

When they arrived in front of his door, my father and my uncle Avdal Khan, tense, shouted "Mushir!" Our cousin climbed up on the roof to escape. My uncle called out to him, "Come and see, we've brought you your coffin."

Mushir, panicked, was stranded on the rooftop. My father added, "You've dishonored the family," and my uncle called him a collaborator and fired on him. The women were still weeping around the coffin. Avdal Khan fired a second shot.

"Why do you go to Mosul so often? To meet whom? The security people? Have you become a spy, Mushir?" Mushir, terrified, tried to hide as best he could. "I'm not a collaborator!" he yelled. My uncle broke down the door, climbed up to the roof with my father tagging behind, and caught Mushir. My father looked at him sadly. "There have been rumors about you for some time . . . We didn't want to believe them . . . But you were never willing to say what you're up to in Mosul. You're out of work yet you always have money. We must avenge the honor of the family . . ." My father was interrupted. My uncle had just fired a bullet into Mushir's knee.

He was on the verge of firing a second time but my father pushed the gun aside with his hand and addressed Mushir again. "If it's true that you're not a collaborator, here, take my gun and fire a bullet into your head! Then we'll believe you. Otherwise we'll have to kill you." Mushir tried to stand erect as best he could. He moaned and pleaded, "I go to Mosul for business!" "What business?" my uncle shouted. My father exhorted him, "Mushir, kill yourself . . . Your coffin is ready . . . We'll make sure you're buried with dignity." As he tried to escape, Mushir was brought to a halt by a bullet fired by my uncle. He fell from the roof, among the women, right near his coffin.

Later it was discovered that Mushir had kept a mistress in Mosul. He had not been a traitor.

The situation was deteriorating from day to day. The number of security officers grew steadily, and the tension kept rising. Trenches were dug around our town and everyone got ready to defend their neighborhood. My father and seven other men mounted guard in a trench opposite the barracks that dominated the town on the little hill behind our orchard. They expected an imminent attack. At the slightest signal from General Barzani, they were ready to launch an assault against the Iraqi barracks. The women and children were to be grouped together in a shelter. My father immediately offered our fortress-house. "I had it built especially for a time like this." No one questioned the sturdiness of the walls in our house, but the problem was its orientation. When it was built, my father had wanted all the windows to face away from the town in the direction of the orchard and the hill overlooking the house. It was a beautiful view. He couldn't have foreseen that within a few months barracks would go up on that hill, a few hundred yards in front of our windows. This was why, to his great sorrow, it was decided that the women and children would go to stay at my uncle Avdal Khan's house.

I didn't want the happiness of this recent period—the joy in the freedom, the concerts, the painting—to disappear. But it was obvious the putsch leaders no longer respected Kurdish rights and Kurdish autonomy. This being the case, I wanted a gun and I wanted to join the men in the trenches. But since there weren't enough weapons to go around, I was put in charge of supplying the fighters. My father and his men were very confident. Their morale was boosted by Voice of America, which referred to us as heroes and freedom fighters. It was truly reassuring to have an ally as important as America. My father kept repeating, "We're Indo-Europeans, like the Americans!" And to reassure himself even more, he added, as his father had, "We're British." Radio Moscow was now treating us as rebels, but we couldn't have cared less: let them "march to socialism" with the Baath Party! Even kids younger than I knew the names Nixon and Kissinger, and we loved them. We stayed in our trenches for several days without anything happening. Then we were given orders to move out of the town because our tanks and airplanes were going to rid the town of all the Iraqi forces and allow us very shortly to return, victorious.

When my mother asked, "Where are the tanks and planes the Americans gave us?" my father said with conviction, "They're hidden in our mountains, and the planes are sheltered in clandestine airports." All of us waited for a sign from the general to march on Kurdistan and liberate it.

That was how we left for the north, for the mountains, convinced we would return, victorious, a month later. It was as though we were leaving on vacation. The roads were congested with vehicles heading north. We stopped for a picnic along the way and arrived in Bijil in the afternoon. Perched on top of our possessions, in the back of the pickup my father had rented, I saw Iraqi policemen captured by our men. As he passed them, my father honked his horn to greet his friend Rajab, from Billē, among the fighters. Rajab returned his greeting, raising his gun in the air. I heard my father, radiant, say to my mother, "You see, we're going to capture all of them, without even firing a shot." Our friend Rajab ran after the pickup and called out to my father, "Shero, we need you desperately. We've retrieved a Morse transmitter at the police station, but those sons of bitches sabotaged it. Come help us repair it!" My father climbed out of the truck and told the driver to continue on with us. I saw him disappear, his old Brno on his shoulder, with his friend. It began to rain.

There was unimaginable chaos in the village of Bijil. The peasants, returning from their pastures with sheep, goats, cows, horses, mingled with countless cars crammed with passengers on their way to the great revolutionary picnic. People and animals were wading through mud, and the rain kept coming down. We were somehow privileged, so my mother, my sisters, my two sisters-in-law—Dijla the villager and Salma the dancer—their children, and I were put up in a room in the house of an acquaintance of my father. My two brothers had gone to join the fighters in the mountains. In spite of all the commotion around me, I felt lonely. The village made me sad. I decided to join my father at the police station, where I found him surrounded by armed men. Facing them were six Iraqi policemen, unarmed and wearing no belts. My father was trying to repair the Morse transmitter; it was connected to a battery, but there were none of the characteristic beeps coming out of the machine. This was the first time I'd seen a transmitter. My father rolled a cigarette and offered it to one of the Iraqis. I was surprised. Then he rolled another one, for himself. He lit it and, looking the policeman straight in the eye, asked, "Tell me . . . What did you do to the machine so that I can't fix it?" The policeman held his head up high. "How could you possibly imagine I sabotaged it?"

I saw my father as a judge. He went on, "If you tell me what you did to this machine, I'll let you and your friends go, unharmed." The policeman shrugged his shoulders and said, "I swear by Allah I didn't touch that machine. I don't know why it doesn't want to work . . ." And to show his goodwill, he tried to help my father repair it. Standing around them, we followed their every gesture very attentively. Rajab, who greatly mistrusted the Iraqis, asked, "What are we going to do with the prisoners if the machine doesn't work?" My father didn't reply; he went outside to smoke a cigarette and calm his nerves, and Rajab followed him. Back inside, my father bent down over the machine again, helped by the policeman, but with no greater success. Rajab marched back into the room like a madman and, aiming his rifle at the policeman's chest, made it clear to him, in broken Arabic, that he was giving him one hour to repair the transmitter, or else he and his companions would be buried along with it. Panicked, the policeman turned to my father and pleaded with him. My father calmed down Rajab, who stepped away, cursing the devil. My father returned to the policeman. "Listen, my brother, I know you sabotaged the machine. Either you repair it immediately or we execute you right away."

The policeman went back to work on the machine, invoking Allah. I saw him tinker with a part. When my father saw that the policeman had started the transmitter going again, he pushed him aside and made a show of repairing the apparatus himself. It started sending out the Morse code again, and my father straightened up, puffing out his chest. "We're proud of you, Shero, the general's operator," Rajab said to him. Then they picked up the secret codes transmitted by the Iraqis and let the policemen go unharmed, advising them to tell our Arab "brothers" that the Kurds weren't enemies of the Iraqis but were simply struggling for their freedom. Our fighters would have liked to keep my father there as their operator, but he declined, declaring, "The general is waiting for me . . ."

When we were back with our family, my father described in great detail how he had fixed the transmitter. I said nothing.

We spent three nights in Bijil, whose population swelled with each new day. Fear of an Iraqi invasion intensified. Bijil was only a stopping point; we were to continue climbing—higher, farther north. We set off again in the direction of Nauperdan, where our leader, Mustafa Barzani, had his headquarters. We were three families traveling on foot. At nightfall, we reached the bank of a wide river. "Is it the Tigris?" I asked my father. "No, my son, it's a tributary, the Zab. Remember? The river where we caught fish in Billē."

At this spot, you could cross the river without swimming, and we first had the women and children go, huddled together on our little group's horse. I was scared of the water, particularly at night. Yet I swam like a fish. Then came my father's turn. With his rifle safe and dry on his shoulders, he clutched the horse's mane and headed into the river. But he was so tense that he hampered the horse, and we saw the current carry them away. We heard my father's cries as the horse thrashed the water furiously with his hoofs. The owner of the horse yelled out, "Let go of his head . . . Hang on to the belongings." We were very frightened. Finally, the men and beasts managed to come out of the river about a hundred yards downstream. And my father, dripping wet, came to dry himself off by the fire.

We parted from the two other families in a village on the riverbank and continued our journey on foot, on horseback, or by car, depending on the opportunities that arose. At long last we arrived in Nauperdan, headquarters of the Kurdish resistance. This was the most protected village in Kurdistan. My brother Rostam was waiting for us there with a house. We felt very important; we were with the families of the top leaders. Our new house, perched on a hill, had only one room. It was a replica of our Billē house. My father was convinced that it had been put at our disposal by the general himself. My brother Rostam set him right and showed him the antiaircraft equipment hidden behind the house. "I'm responsible for the antiaircraft defense, I've got to be operational twenty-four hours a day. That's why I was given this house on the hill." My father went down to headquarters, where the general's secretary warmly welcomed him and my father explained he was at the general's disposal.

There was much activity in the village, with *peshmergas* coming and going incessantly. Iraq had just launched a large-scale offensive. Our town of Aqra and all the other towns in Kurdistan had fallen into the hands of the Iraqis, and hundreds of thousands of people had taken to the roads and were converging northward. But our faith was unshakable. America was behind us, and so was Iran, its ally. Our radio station, Voice of Kurdistan, kept us informed of events hour by hour. The newscaster spoke in an impassioned voice of the heroic resistance of our troops. My father then listened very attentively to Voice of America, which called us "freedom fighters." And then it was the turn of Radio Moscow, which called us vulgar rebels, acting against Saddam Hussein, "champion of socialism!" But my father wasn't worried. America and Henry Kissinger were on our side.

War or no war, life continued, and I had to go back to school. I was very happy because classes were once again in Kurdish, and I became an active member of the Kurdish Youth Association. A young officer from the resistance gave us political education classes after school. He always wore an impeccable Kurdish suit, and on his hip he sported a gun with a white-plated butt. He began his classes by writing on the blackboard: "1946: creation of the Kurdish Democratic Party, birth of the Kurdish Republic. Capital: Mahābād." Then he wrote the word *democracy*, separating each syllable. "DE-MO-CRA-CY." He always repeated, "This is a Greek word which means government by the people." He would draw a large map for us, with Turkey in the north, Iraq in the south, Iran in the east, and Syria in the west. In the center, with red chalk, he drew a crescent-shaped country, Kurdistan. He explained how the British and French had divided our country into four parts, and in the course of his demonstration he enlarged the Kurdish territory, adding a half inch here and half inch there. Then he drew a blue heart on Kurdistan and cut it into four parts. "This is how the heart of the Kurds is broken apart." His words were beautiful, and they made me melancholy.

I met Jian. She was even more ravishing than the girls in the Indian films I used to watch on my uncle's television. She didn't dress like the other girls. She wore jeans and big sweaters, and she had snow boots. We knew that her father was an important person and that he went abroad often, particularly to America. She was so beautiful that the boys didn't dare approach her, except for Sertchil. He was also well dressed and had an important father. No one had the courage to compete with Sertchil, who threatened anyone who got near Jian. But I didn't care because Jian was interested in me. One day Sertchil and I scuffled. I had to change classes, and Jian followed me. I always left for school early to meet her.

One Monday, on the little bridge where the Nauperdan checkpoint had been set up, I heard gunshots and saw a man fall under a hail of bullets. The gunman was immediately arrested and headquarters ordered him killed right then, at the scene of the crime. A man was chosen to execute the sentence. I was convinced the killer was a collaborator and therefore deserved his punishment. But I was surprised to see he showed no fear. Unable to bear his gaze, the fighter who was supposed to execute him told him to turn around. The man refused. "No, I won't turn around." The fighter insisted, then ended up firing two bullets, one into the man's head, the other straight into his heart. I applauded along with everyone else, yelling, "Long live Kurdistan! Long live the general!"

Then I learned that this man had not been a collaborator. He had killed to avenge his honor. For me, only traitors to the cause deserved execution.

I arrived late to my appointment with Jian, regretting that I had applauded.

Jian and I had been selected to sing in a choir that was to accompany the singer Mahmad Shekho, a tall, thin man who wore eyeglasses with thick lenses. His accompanist was a young musician whose name was Timar. They were Kurds from Syria who had joined our movement to champion the Kurdish cause. This was the first time I'd seen Kurds from the other parts of Kurdistan—physicians, engineers, performers, artists, all kinds of people who came from territories occupied by Turkey, Iran, and Syria. Mahmad Shekho repeated constantly that our country couldn't be liberated just with guns, that we also needed violins and drums. And we recorded many songs for our radio station, Voice of Kurdistan.

Winter arrived, snow began to fall, and I saw more and more wounded and dead brought in on mules and in trucks. And still our planes didn't fly from our clandestine airports.

One night, we heard low-flying Iraqi planes overhead and our window broke into pieces. We rushed outside. Someone started screaming, "They're our planes! Don't fire!" My brother Rostam and his comrades directed hails of antiaircraft fire at the planes. They knew full well they weren't ours. One plane was hit and burst into flames. We cheered loudly and the planes disappeared without bombing us.

The sky became calm again; we all went down to congratulate and embrace Rostam and his companions. I was fascinated by this brother who reigned over his antiaircraft battery.

As for my father, he continued to work on Morse code signals in the military office and still waited to be summoned by the general. It didn't dawn on him that there were now much more efficient operators than he in Barzani's employ . . .

The planes returned. I was at school. We all rushed outside and went to hide in the trenches that had been dug in case of air raids. I wanted to hold Jian in my arms and protect her, but I was too shy. I looked at her, I looked at the sky; napalm bombs were falling all around us.

When calm returned, we gathered around our teacher. "When will our airplanes be called in?" "They'll be called in, they'll be called in . . ." said our teacher with a sad smile.

When I got home, I asked my father, "Papa, we were supposed to have left for a one-month picnic . . ." But my father turned his head away.

Soon there were bombardments every day. Our schedules were disrupted: school now started at nightfall. We would huddle around the oil lamp to listen to our lessons; it was very cold. After school, Jian walked home with me in the dark. The ground was covered with snow, and above us the black sky was studded with stars. Jian had a flashlight to light up the road. One night, as I was shivering with cold, she took a bar of chocolate out of her coat and we nibbled on it.

I found my parents at home, warming themselves around the stove. They hadn't eaten anything and they sent me out to get bread at the *peshmergas'* baker. We were entitled to two free loaves of bread per day, per person. My mother prepared tea. Rostam came to share the meal with us, then he retired with his young wife behind my father's long turban, which had been unrolled and hung up to protect their intimacy.

Jian gave me one of her anoraks and a flashlight. The whole class envied me. Jian loved me, and I loved her as much as I loved Kurdistan. Now, thanks to Jian, at night, during recess, I could take part in the flashlight competition, to see whose light could be beamed the farthest.

Then the school had to close down: there were air bombardments day and night, and still no planes of ours in the sky. We started to lose hope.

The headquarters withdrew even farther north and we had to abandon the house. We went to hide in two huge caves, one for women, the other for men. There were no more days or nights. Between bombings, I would somehow manage to meet Jian. My father sent Morse code messages uninterruptedly from the men's cave. We were surrounded by wounded people who had to be cared for with inadequate means. Those killed in the bombings were buried immediately. I helped the nurses and slept with my father's Morse code beeping on one side and the moans of the wounded on the other. As I was getting up to go see Jian, a wounded man next to me was moaning his children's names, then suddenly stopped. He had just died. I scratched the nape of my neck and found blood on my fingertips. I scratched myself again and realized I was covered with lice. This was even more unpleasant than the worms of the Zab River. I ran to the women's cave to find my mother and show her what was happening to me. She smiled on seeing me so upset, then I saw her eyes fill with tears. She led me to the edge of a stream and washed my clothes while I shivered, wrapped in a big blanket. She sheared me like a lamb, and I didn't go see Jian.

Word went out that Iraq and Iran were about to conclude a treaty, at our expense, with Kissinger's consent.

On the Kurdish radio station, a poem was declaimed describing the heavenly beauty of our mountains and the pure water of our rivers, the Tigris and the Euphrates. But I was no longer a kid. The mountains I saw were harsh, the rivers full of worms, and the sky saturated with napalm bombs.

We received orders for the women, children, and old people to head for the Iranian frontier. We could no longer think things through rationally or soundly. A mortal solitude swept over our people. We were being betrayed by the Americans as we had been previously betrayed by the Soviets. On a beautiful March day, Saddam Hussein of Iraq signed a treaty with the shah of Iran;* we were losing our last support. A long letter by General Barzani addressed to Kissinger, begging him to keep his promise, was read over our radio, but Kissinger abandoned us to our fate.

*March 6, 1975, in Algiers.

I went to the *peshmergas'* baker, but there was no longer anyone there. There was nothing but our clandestine radio station still broadcasting appeals to the entire world—Jesus, Muhammad, Gandhi, Buddha, Abraham Lincoln—to come to the aid of our people. I saw some *peshmergas* commit suicide in despair. Others wanted to hide in the mountains and resist, but the general understood we were caught in an inescapable net: the choice was between accepting defeat or extermination. We took the road of exile.

Along with other families, we piled into a truck bound for the Iranian frontier; there was no alternative. After several kilometers, we climbed out of the truck, exhausted, our bundles of belongings on our shoulders. We crossed the frontier under the supervision of the Iranian police and were herded up a small hill where we sat on our heels, surrounded by soldiers. I felt as if I were in a cemetery, with all those people around me, the crouching women in their dark dresses, their heads buried in their knees, weeping. We were annihilated, and I started to cry. We were taken to a camp made up of tents. It was a gift from the United Nations. We were refugees.

Then the men arrived, heads lowered, defeated—among them my two brothers and my father, General Barzani's personal operator. Out of fear of Savak, the Iranian secret police, we couldn't cry out against the Iranians' betrayal of us.

Dozens of refugee camps stretched along the Iranian border. We were forbidden to go out without a Savak safe-conduct. And yet this land, too, was Kurdish; it was one of the quarters of our heart according to the sketch of our young teacher in Nauperdan. I set about looking for Jian, without success. Passing by a tent, I heard a man moan:

it was Timar, one of the Kurdish musicians from Syria. It started to rain; our camp became a field of mud.

The summer went by with its blazing heat, and then winter came, bitingly cold that year.

We were moved to another camp. We now lived in long sheds with small square cells giving out on a central passageway; each family was assigned a cell. Time stood still; we had nothing to do. A few boys and I would leave the shed and walk around and around inside the camp, like dogs. Once, I spotted my brother Dilovan standing apart with some friend. I wanted to go up to him, but he signaled me to keep away; they were getting drunk.

That evening, when I returned, I saw Dilovan stretched out in his cell. He was hiccuping, and tears streamed from his closed eyes. He howled continually: "I want to go back and fight in our mountains." He threw up in a saucepan and his wife wiped his mouth. Day in, day out, this was a recurring scene, for him and for others.

Classes started again. I still wanted to be a judge or a lawyer, and I was still looking for Jian. But deep down I knew I would never see her—or Kurdistan—again.

Passing in front of the corner of the shed where my uncle Avdal Khan and his family lived, I heard someone singing and playing the *saz*, the beautiful Kurdish lute. I went to look, and found Mahmad Shekho, the other singer from Syria with whom Jian and I had recorded songs for Voice of Kurdistan. He was scrawnier than before, but his voice hadn't changed; it was still just as beautiful as ever. He smiled at me, and I went out of the room, haunted by the words of his song: "The more time goes by, the more my heart beats slowly, my beloved . . ."

My father gave me a bit of pocket money. I and a slightly older friend got passes for a few hours and went to Mahābād: Mahābād, the city that had been the capital of the

Kurdish Republic, where Mustafa Barzani had become general in 1946; but also the city where the Kurdish president Qazi Mohammed had been hanged by the Iranians barely one year later, in March 1947.

Everyone spoke Kurdish in Mahābād, but no one ever discussed politics; fear reigned. A banner read, "The shah's orders are God's orders." We stopped to eat a kebab and the owner of the little restaurant wouldn't let us pay; he understood we were refugees, defeated Kurds. My friend, who was very talkative, asked the owner, "Why don't you fight against the shah to liberate this part of Kurdistan?" After a long, thoughtful pause, the owner answered, scratching his head, "If the shah orders us to, we shall obey." The owner told us there was a movie theater in town, so we decided to go. They were showing an Iranian film. When I saw the image appear on the screen, I got very excited, and once again I vowed to myself that, someday, I would bring Kurds to the screen.

Savak summoned all the Kurds in the camp to come and listen to an Iraqi minister who had arrived by helicopter to tell us that an amnesty had been granted and we could go home. We didn't believe him; we thought it was a trap. Who could possibly trust the Baghdad putsch leaders? The Baathist minister was booed, then everything degenerated: his leg was broken and soon he was covered in blood. I was in a rage, and I punched the minister along with the others. Then the Savak men fired into the crowd and killed twelve people. Helped away by his bodyguards, the minister took off in his helicopter, in a cloud of spit and insults. After this visit, everyone did start to wonder: what indeed were we doing here, closely watched refugees, in this camp, with no future?

Some families managed to obtain visas to the United States, others to Canada. Why wouldn't we emigrate as well? My father held a family council to consider the question.

Each of us imagined himself already in America—my father a journalist, my mother a supermarket manager, my brother a general, and I making a great Kurdish film. Then my mother started talking about her brothers, her orchard, and her pomegranate trees; my father brought up his fortress-house, his friends, his land; and I thought about my partridges, my cousin Cheto's pigeons, my school, and my river. Soon we were all weeping.

That settled the matter; we would go home. And my father concluded, "It's more honorable to die on our own land than to become American immigrants or militiamen working for the shah." We gathered our meager belongings. I went to pick up my school certificate and we set off for the border.

On the road there were many families, like us, going to give themselves up to the Iraqi authorities. Our small truck came to a stop; we climbed out and, after loading our skimpy bundles on our backs and walking past the Iranian soldiers, we crossed through a no-man's-land of about a hundred yards between the two armies. In the distance we heard the Iranians bid us farewell, but we didn't have the courage to turn around; we were already under the watchful eye of the Iraqi army. At the frontier a large banner awaited us: "Welcome to the land of the Mother Country." Iraqi officers and soldiers awaiting us approached and helped us carry our belongings. Behind us, our people still on the Iranian side of the border watched attentively to see how we were being welcomed, and turning around furtively, I saw several of them follow in our footsteps. Still escorted by the soldiers, we made our way down a small hill, and Iran disappeared from our view. Instantly the behavior of the soldiers changed. They threw our bundles into a military truck and ordered us to get in. Two soldiers flanked us, their weapons cocked at us. And I thought of the image of partridges used as hunting bait to attract their fellow creatures. This is what we had become, and I felt guilty. We had served as bait; the others would follow us and suffer the same fate. After about a half mile, the truck pulled over and we were ordered to get out with our hands on our heads. We had to jump from the high floor of the truck; my mother fell to the ground and a soldier yelled at her to stand up at once. Then, surrounded by military personnel, the men and women were separated. We were taken to a building where we were ordered to undress. We were embarrassed, but under threat of the soldiers, we had no choice. I ended up next to my father, naked, with my hands on my head. I didn't dare look at him. While the soldiers were searching every fold of our garments, my father, humiliated, was hiding his genitals with his hands, his legs trembling with shame. A soldier forced him to put his hands on his head; then, using his bayonet, he made him spread his legs apart and, jabbing him with his weapon, made him pivot. When the search was over, we were allowed to put our clothes back on. Filled with shame, I thought about my mother, my sisters, my sisters-in-law, and what they were being subjected to, and I began to think it might have been better to die in the Iranian camps than be reduced to this. In the next building, an officer waited for us with our papers, which he seemed to ignore. We had to state our names, and our dates and places of birth. When it came to "profession," I was curious to see what my father would say. For the first time, he didn't give his usual proud answer, "I'm the general's personal operator." He said, "Baker." Then it was our turn to state our occupations: student for Rostam and me, teacher for Dilovan, my older brother. Full of contempt, the officer called us asses for having believed in America and for having challenged Baathist Iraq.

And for our crazy dreams of Kurdistan.

We went into another room for identity photos. We were

all together again, men and women, and I saw my mother in front of the camera, her face under the lights. She sat in profile, presenting her right side. The military photographer ordered her to face the camera, but she didn't move. He repeated his command, in vain: she didn't understand Arabic. He went up to her and turned her head: she was blind in her left eye, which had a spot in the shape of a white cloud. Her face was pale and expressionless. When the photo session was over, we returned to the first officer. He took fingerprints of each of us, on the bottom of a blank sheet, and we were ordered to wait outside.

We sat on the ground, under the triumphant gazes of the Iraqi soldiers. In my mind's eye I saw the barbed wire at the frontier, behind the hill, and another family crossing it, as we had a short while ago. My father, turning unobtrusively to my mother, whispered in her ear, "And what if we escaped to the United States?" My mother didn't even bother responding. Rostam, glancing at the soldiers around us, asked, "How?" "It's still possible; the border is right in front of us," said my father. "Once we get there, we go to Tehran, straight to the American embassy." My older brother Dilovan, who was sketching in the earth with a twig, head down, said only, "It's over, Papa, we've lost everything." My father took out his tobacco pouch and rolled himself a cigarette.

A soldier arrived and ordered us to follow him. He led us to an office where a man in civvies was waiting for us, a pistol lying on his desk. He was holding a stack of papers. He counted us, called out our names, then handed the papers to my father. "Here are your new papers, you can leave." My father took the papers and, incredulous, asked, "We can leave?" "Yes, go home." And we left his office. We retrieved our belongings and a soldier pointed to some waiting taxis. After a last check, we piled into a taxi and set off for Aqra.

During the trip, my father looked at our new papers:

photo, name, place of birth, and one word stamped in red across the entire page: *aïdoun*.★ At the entrance to Aqra, while the police were checking our papers, I caught sight of a huge banner above our heads with portraits of President al-Bakr and Vice President Saddam Hussein on each side, announcing, "*oumma Arabia wahida zat. Risaala khalida*," "The Arab nation is one. It is the bearer of a divine message."

★Literally, "fallen back into line." —Translator's note

This time, no one in our neighborhood came to welcome us as they had in 1970. No one ran to embrace us or escort us to our house. The house was still standing, but it was occupied. Children were playing in front of the door. A man and a woman came out; we introduced ourselves as the owners. The man replied that he had no knowledge of this. "But this house is ours," said my father. "Come back tomorrow, we'll discuss it," the man said. Three months went by and this man and his family went on living in our house.

We moved into my uncle Avdal Khan's house, the uncle with the television. He was still in the camps in Iran. I pictured him with Mahmad Shekho, the tall, skinny singer and *saz* player, singing songs of hope that were swept away by the wind.

When he died, his family had to surrender to the Iraqis in order to be able to bury him, out of respect, on his land. We then had to give his house back to my aunt, his widow, and their six children.

So my father returned to see the man who was still occupying our house. My father looked him in the eye. "Brother, this house belongs to me. I built it with my own hands," he said, showing the palms of his hands, "and with my children's help. My previous house was torn down and set on fire. This one is in my blood. I plan to die here. I'm an *aï-doun*, but you listen to me: even if you have the entire Iraqi government on your side, if you haven't cleared out in a week, I'll kill you." Three days later our house was vacated.

I resumed my adolescent life. One day, with my cousin Cheto and some other friends, we went to the cemetery to gather almonds, but not a single one remained on the almond tree; you'd think the dead had eaten them all. There was a bare hill overlooking the cemetery, where we spotted Slo's donkey. The donkey was roaming free; he had become useless, he was scrawny and sick, abandoned by Slo, fated to be devoured by a wolf or a wild dog. He had climbed halfway up the hill to get to the leaves of the one tree on the slope, but he had fallen just before reaching the tree. We got closer. He was struggling to get back on his feet. We pushed him up to the top of the hill. Cheto stood aside; he knew what we were about to do, but he could do nothing to check our violent impulses.

When we reached the top of the hill, we threw the donkey down into the ravine and laughed at the sight of the poor creature rolling to the bottom. Cheto was heartsick but tried to hide his sorrow, hoping to be spared our sarcastic remarks. To tease him we brought up his stunt pigeons. Ramo answered for him, "That time's over, the time of the stunt pigeons . . . Now, it's *Dilma*."★ Cheto had replaced the pigeons with a she-cat; for us, a she-cat was a woman's animal. It was our belief that since his father's—my uncle's—murder, poor Cheto, who was an only son, was far too spoiled by the women in his house—his mother, his two sisters, and his two aunts.

Having let off some steam, we hurtled down the hill and all of us climbed an enormous white mulberry tree to stuff

★The Disappointed Female. —Translator's note

ourselves with fruit. When we were sated, we began crushing the fruit on our genitals and jerking off, competing to see who would ejaculate fastest. This was the first time I masturbated, and it was Zorab who won.

My school certificate covering the period I had spent in the mountains and in Iran was not approved, and I was back in the same school, in the same classroom, on the same bench. I was four years behind. I had to take my classes over again in Arabic. I passed my final exam and could finally enter high school. I was given new books with a photo of the president on the first page, and on the back cover the inevitable inscription: *oumma Arabia* . . . "The Arab nation is one . . ." My school had changed its name. It was no longer the Peace School; it had become the Baath School. Next to the headmaster's office, there was a room occasionally occupied by a man with a thick, drooping mustache, the distinctive feature of Baath Party members; he met with Baathist students there. The whole school was getting ready to celebrate the tenth anniversary of the party's rise to power. I was summoned to the office of the man with the thick mustache. A "Do Not Enter" sign was posted on his door. I found myself with several classmates; he made us sing one by one, in order to select the best voices. When my turn came, he noticed that I didn't know a single Arabic song and ordered me to leave. I went—delighted. But he called me back almost immediately and, pointing at me, ordered me to get my hair cut. "Young Iraqis must be clean and disciplined." As soon as school was out, I ran to the barber, Abdulla the Communist. The painting of the young Kurdish girl was no longer hanging opposite the mirror; it had been replaced by a large photograph of the president. In the entire town, I couldn't find a single work by the painter Sami. As for Sami himself, I would sometimes come across him at a specific spot in the center of town: he would be standing on one leg, leaning back against the wall, a cigarette between his lips, contemplating the town for hours. When the cigarette was no more than a butt, he'd take it out of his mouth with a slow gesture and stub it on the ground. Passersby would greet him quickly, as though reluctant to disturb his thoughts, and he would calmly reply, "*roj bash*," hello. Whenever I saw him, I'd stand a bit removed, off to one side, inconspicuously, and follow his gaze. He always stared at the same things: clothes drying on clotheslines, the shiny sheet-metal water containers on the rooftops, featureless people sadly going into and out of their houses. What could he have been thinking about for all those hours, looking at such sights?

He would walk off with short steps and melt into the crowd.

I started painting again. I wanted to become a great painter, like Sami. The school was organizing an exhibition, so I brought over some of my best canvases. I was very excited to take part in this exhibition. On the day before the opening, I was summoned by the official in charge. One of my paintings was propped up against the wall: it represented a chained man raising his eyes to the sky.

I recalled that when I had initially painted this picture, the figure had the same skin color as I, but dissatisfied with the color, I had repainted the skin black. The official in charge of the exhibition wanted to know why I had painted such a skinny man. "You make it look as if Iraqis are dying of hunger. And why those chains? What's the significance of that?" To cover myself, I replied, "He isn't Iraqi, he's African." He ordered me to paint other subjects: the accomplishments of the Baath Party, the nationalization of oil, the Palestinian struggle against Zionism and imperialism. "I'm still a young painter," I replied. "I haven't had time to paint all those subjects, but I'll surely get around to it." My paintings were returned to me. I was rejected for the exhibition.

It was a warm day in late spring 1979. I saw my father hurrying home. His eyes were sparkling, and as was his habit, before even reaching the entrance to the house he was unrolling his belt while walking. I hadn't seen him so worked up since we had become *aïdouns*. I could tell that something was happening. When he was right near the house, he called out to my mother. As soon as she appeared at the doorstep, he threw her his belt and drew her inside. "Haybet," he said, "there are people who have returned to the mountains to fight!" My mother stopped in her tracks, astounded. I thought she would regard this as marvelous news, but I was wrong. "What's the point?" she said, and there was a long silence. Then my father came up to me, finger raised. "Listen to me carefully, my son. What you've just heard must not get out. If the government has any suspicions, we'll be in great danger. We're *aïdouns*, we're all suspect."

As *aïdouns*, we were denied access to many jobs—at the university, in the government, or in any sensitive position. But in fact the rule was applied to all Kurds. If a person pronounced so much as one word that displeased the government, he would disappear. The mosques were called "Baathist mosques," and so were the streets, the neighborhoods, the hills; everything was now "Baathist," even the brothels. Everyone lived according to the proverb "Hold on to your hat so the wind won't blow it away."

Hundreds of thousands of workers from all the Arab countries moved into our region. They took up the jobs that were vacated by the ousting of *aïdouns* and many other Kurds. With the victory of *oumma Arabia*, our country became a tourist paradise for Iraqis and Arabs from the Gulf countries; they came to our mountains to relax. Large hotels, camping sites, and villas sprouted everywhere. The Kurds had been crushed once and for all. Arab tourists strolled down the streets in djellabas, throwing contemptuous glances our way often enough. Some Western tourists also came, but they were escorted by the *mokhabarat*★ to ensure they had no contact with us. Our town became a bit livelier, but we were demoralized.

I decided to leave Aqra during the summer holiday. I was curious about everything, and I went to look for work in the region around Dihok, where there had been no tourists before the Kurdish insurrection. I heard that a movie theater in Sarsing was looking for a projectionist. I hurried there: for me there was no more appealing job. I could see films, which would be an initial apprenticeship. I was received by a tall, dark-haired man. I couldn't fool anyone with my Kurdish accent in Arabic. He asked me quietly, "Are you from the Patriotic Union of Kurdistan or from the Kurdish Democratic Party?"† He expected to trip me up. I was dealing with someone from the intelligence service. I replied as quietly as he, "I'm a student." Someone called out to him from the far end of the screening room and he left, giving me an appointment in the afternoon. I decided not to go back, and disappeared in the town.

The streets were crowded—I saw happy Arab children enjoying the tourist paradise; the Kurds sold fruit juices and refreshing yogurt on the sidewalks. I left Sarsing and went to Anichkē, where there was a camping site with trailers. I became the assistant of a Kurdish electrician who was employed by the government. We were given lodgings in Soulav, in a luxury state-owned hotel perched on a hill and

★Iraqi secret police. —Translator's note
†The PUK, founded in 1975 and led by Jalal Talabani, and the KDP, led by Barzani, were feuding Kurdish forces throughout this period.

surrounded by mountains. I shared a room with a man who always listened to the same cassette, played very loudly. I was an assistant electrician, but I had to do a multitude of other tasks—cleaning the swimming pool, helping in the kitchen . . . Everything there belonged to the state, and we were the state's employees.

Summoned to fix the electricity in a trailer, I was received by two fifty- or sixty-year-old men from Baghdad. They were drinking raki under a tree. As I got nearer I saw their hair was dyed. They were clearly rich; perhaps they were high-level government employees . . . Pointing to the trailer, they explained what was wrong, and I went over to it with my toolbox. Inside the trailer, I saw a very handsome boy, around ten years old, lying on a large bed. He was staring up at the ceiling with his big eyes. I did my repairs without exchanging a word with him. When I came out, one of the two men from Baghdad, suspicious, stood up and went to the caravan to check on the boy. Then they invited me to join them for a drink because I was young as well. I turned them down, with a perfunctory smile, my heart filled with hatred.

Upon returning to the hotel, I found my roommate stretched out, listening to his music as loud as ever. While I was taking my shower, a hotel employee came to fetch me. The manager wanted to see us. This did not put my mind at ease. He was a party member, of course; I sometimes would see him with a group of men and women, always at the same table by the swimming pool, facing my country's magnificent landscape. Seeing him savor that natural beauty made me jealous. It was as if the hills and mountains were my sisters and he was mentally undressing them.

It was at 7:30 p.m., on July 14, 1979, when I went downstairs, reminding my roommate that the manager was expecting us. He didn't react at all, still absorbed in his music: "She left her father's house to go to the neighbors'.

She walked by without greeting me. Perhaps my beauty is angry . . ."

I tore down the stairs like a criminal. Perhaps I was under suspicion? Perhaps someone had informed on me for some trivial reason? I went into the big reception room where all the hotel employees were assembled. I was surprised; everyone except the manager looked cheerful, and there were many bottles of champagne on the tables. My first thought was of a marriage or birthday. My roommate arrived last, and leaned against the wall near the door. The manager, wearing a green suit, opened his arms, invited us to take our seats, and then seated himself. I still had no idea why I'd been summoned. I looked at him, in suspense; he was searching for his words. Finally he began, "This evening, at eight o'clock p.m., President Ahmed Hassan al-Bakr—" As soon as we heard the president's name, we applauded mechanically, but the manager stopped us "—resigned." A hush fell over the room. My immediate thought was that there had been a coup d'état, but the manager continued his speech, "And Vice President Saddam Hussein has become president." We didn't know whether we were meant to applaud or not. He looked at his watch and switched on the television. We saw al-Bakr appear on the screen. He repeated almost word for word what the manager had just said and finished by saying, "May the people and the Baathists remain loyal to the new president." We had never seen the president look so downcast. We had known for a long time that President al-Bakr would have been happy to have the power his vice president had.

Then it was the new president's turn to take over the screen. Saddam Hussein's portrait was accompanied by the newscaster's excited commentary, followed by anthems to the glory of the Baath Party and the "divine message" of the Arab nation. The champagne bottles were uncorked to the beat of this martial music. I was tasting champagne for the first time; it was a gift of the Baath Party made at the wish of the new president. While we were drinking, the manager went out. There were some large portraits of the former and new presidents in the hotel. Immediately after the "cocktail," we were ordered to take down all the portraits of al-Bakr. I was well acquainted with the new president; since 1968 my father's radio station had been referring to Saddam as "the gangster from Tikrit." I had grown up with him. No one made the slightest comment as we returned to our rooms. We had already been afraid of him when he was vice president; now that he was president, the wisest thing to do was to fall into a deep slumber.

Ten days before the end of my work term, I was dismissed: I didn't have a Baathist Youth card. This made me rather happy. I missed my family—it was the first time I had lived far apart from them—and I set off for home after a very busy summer.

When school started, we had a new math teacher. As soon as I saw him I assumed he was an Arab and a Baathist. I put my elbows on my desk and buried my head in my hands. Damn, I said to myself, I'm already hopeless in math; with this guy, I'm sunk! He paced in front of the blackboard and introduced himself: "My name is Jacob." Then we called out our names one by one. Without looking at us, and still pacing in front of the blackboard, he asked, "What dialect do you speak?" I was convinced his question was a trap. No one responded. Unable to suppress my patriotism, I said dryly, "It's not a question of dialects. We're Kurds, that's all." The teacher stopped pacing. "Calm down, brother! I'm a Kurd too." We were all amazed; we looked at him, incredulous. The following day, my doubts were dispelled when I saw him strolling with Jamil, one of my brother Dilovan's friends.

Every time my brother came home, he and Jamil would spend hours talking together in the safety of our orchard about the struggle, and about the fact that aside from their mountains, the Kurds had no friends. Being an *aïdoun*, Dilovan wasn't allowed to teach. He had been forced to look for a new job, and had found work with a tailor who did alterations in Erbil.

I hadn't been wrong about Jacob; it's true he had wanted to know our political leanings, but his intentions were good. I now saw him as a very brave man, for a great many people in the schools worked for the Baath Party. Before long we became friends, and he invited me to his house, and lent me books by George Bernard Shaw and Régis Debray. I would have one week to read them; other readers were waiting their turn, for these books were forbidden. I also read Gorky's *Mother* and Sartre's *Being and Nothingness* from cover to cover, without understanding a word (nor had the Arabic translator, probably), and I was a week late in returning them. For me, reading these forbidden books was a patriotic duty. I devoured Jack London's *The Iron Heel* and learned that Che Guevara had changed his first name to Ernesto in homage to its hero. In the process I discovered the French Revolution and Nehru's *Glimpses of World History*, where the Kurds are discussed. We readers from this underground circle recognized each other from certain turns of phrases and words, but we had to remain very discreet. Jacob started inserting pamphlets between the pages of the books he lent me; I was aware of the danger involved, of course, and knew that if just a single pamphlet was found on my body it could cost me my life. The Baath Party was watching. Our crazy dream of Kurdish independence lived on. We were recovering from the defeat of 1975. Underground networks were regrouping.

One day, Jacob asked me if I had the courage to fire a few shots. I assured him I did. He gave me a loaded sixteen-shot pistol with a long barrel. It was even older and rustier than my father's Brno. I thought it probably wouldn't work. Jacob advised me to test it before using it: "Just fire a bullet into a wet pillow." I took the pistol, wrapped it up in a sheet of newspaper, slipped it into an ordinary plastic bag, and, before going home, covered it by filling up the bag with tomatoes. One of the streets I had to take had Baath Party offices on one side and residences of Baathist employees on the other. I was always unsure where to look when I walked on that street since I didn't want to arouse suspicion. I started walking, but when I reached the party office building, someone called out to me from the front steps. I turned my head and saw one of my teachers, who was a Baathist official. The way he called out to me was not like a teacher calling out to a student but like an officer calling out to a soldier. He walked up to me and asked me some ordinary questions. "How are you? What's new in the world?" While I answered with something like "Everything's fine," I was figuring out how much time I would need, should he go beyond mere questions, to pull out my weapon and kill him, how long it would take me to run to the orchards, which I knew like the back of my hand, and what roads to take so I wouldn't be impeded in my getaway. But he only glanced briefly at my plastic bag, lingered by my side for a minute, which seemed an eternity, and headed back to the office building. My heart slowly stopped pounding. When I got home, I went directly to our orchard to bury the pistol under a pomegranate tree. Several days later I returned to the place where I had hidden it because the day was approaching when I would need to use it. I noticed right away that the earth had been dug up. Yet the pistol was still there. My brother Rostam came to me and said, "If you people need anyone, count me in." He had discovered my hiding place when he had gone to water the trees.

When the day came, I returned to the orchard. My brother Dilovan and his friend Jamil were there. I had to wait for them to leave. Time went by. They didn't move, and the hour of the meeting was drawing nearer. Finally they left, but I no longer had time to test the weapon. I grabbed it and ran. At 8 p.m. sharp, I was in front of the restaurant where the head security officer went drinking every evening. Another schoolmate was waiting at the spot chosen for our assassination attempt. As soon as he saw that we were in our assigned positions, my teacher Jacob, who could pass for an Arab, entered into the walled area around the restaurant. He was supposed to let us know if the head security officer was really in the garden. We were then supposed to jump over the wall and kill him. We were waiting for the signal to go into action when I saw a fourth accomplice arrive on the scene; he ordered us to stop everything: the restaurant was surrounded by plainclothes policemen.

My brother Dilovan and his friend Jamil disappeared. My sister-in-law was the only person in on their secret. Three months later, on my father's old Russian radio, we heard my brother calling out, in a moving voice, "Voice of Kurdistan speaking—" It was the pirate radio station of the resistance. And once again I heard the national anthem *Ey Raquib* . . . "Oh my friends, be assured the Kurdish people are alive and nothing can bring down their flag . . ." But this time my father didn't say, "In a year we'll be free," as he usually did. He switched the radio off, disillusioned, and we were fearful: my brother's voice could be recognized by anyone who knew him, and this was very dangerous for us all. As my mother put it, we were "in the eye of the hurricane." So whenever a neighbor told us he had heard my brother, we fiercely denied it was he; we feared denunciations.

At school, I was summoned to the office with the "Do Not Enter" sign on the door. The man from the security forces made me sit down and asked me straight off, "So when do you plan to sign up with the Baathist Youth?" "It's a good organization, but I've never thought about the question," I said. "Listen, the school, the books, the notebooks are all gifts of the party, which does everything for all of you. We must be loyal to the party and its principles." Scratching the fuzz beginning to grow on my chin, I thought desperately about how to extricate myself from this situation. Watching me, he asked, "What's that you have? A Ho Chi Minh beard?" I played innocent. "Him, I don't know; it's more like a Leonardo da Vinci beard." Before letting me leave, he added, "We're patient, you still have a bit of time to think about it." At the door he stopped me and said neutrally, "Don't forget we know who your brother is." I was crushed. So the security people knew that my brother was the announcer on the new radio station of the Kurdish resistance. I realized my days in school were numbered. But that wasn't the worst of it.

A new presidential decree stipulated that any eighteen-year-old without a degree would have to leave for military service. I was still in school, and since I was four years behind it was easy to calculate that I wouldn't have my diploma by the time I was eighteen. Now I would never become a judge or a lawyer.

My father knew a government employee at the town hall who was in charge of the registry office. He gathered all my papers and we set off for the town hall. At the market he purchased two plump roosters, and we continued on our way.

When we came to the employee, we sat down with the two roosters at our feet, and the discussion started. "What can I do for you, Mr. Shero?" Leaning toward him, my father began. "Four years before my son's birth, Azad here present, I had a son with the same first name who died. When this one was born, I called him Azad, and since the two boys had the same first name, we used all the first child's papers for the second one. At the time, the problems of age, school, and military service never crossed my mind. Now I'd like to set the record straight by obtaining a death certificate for the first Azad and a birth certificate for this one, who is very much alive. He must be made four years younger."

The employee deliberated for a long time, opened old registers, turned pages, stood up, and closed the book. "It's very difficult to make one son die and give birth to this one." My father resumed. "Listen, I have two dreams in my life: I won't tell you what the first is [I could easily guess]; the second is that I'd like to see my son go to university and become a judge or a lawyer. And now I'll die without either of my wishes coming true." The employee lit a cigarette. My father realized that two roosters were insufficient. Standing up, he got closer to the employee, then reached into his pocket and handed him a pair of earrings. "Look, here is the last gold jewelry we have." As he put them in the employee's hand he added, "Do something." Glancing quickly at the earrings, the employee put them away in his drawer. "Come back tomorrow, Mr. Shero, I'll see what I can do . . ." We left our papers with him. My father signaled me to take the two roosters, and before leaving he said, "Tell my son where your house is." When I returned to the same office the next day, I saw my date of birth had been changed from 1960 to 1964, and I heard the employee whisper to my father, "I'm a good Kurdish patriot." I thought, Roosters or patriotism, who cares, my problem is solved.

Halfway home, my father signaled me to stop. He was tired and sat down to rest. He rolled himself a cigarette, and for the first time, I noticed my father had aged. I was very touched by my parents' sacrifice: they had given away my mother's last gold earrings so that I could pursue my studies. We started walking again. I laughed and said to him, "Papa, the employee changed my date of birth because he knows you were the general's personal operator." He looked at me, and his face lit up with a small smile. Then he swallowed, fell silent for a long time, and said gently, "My son, you must go to university. But I don't want you to become a judge or a lawyer anymore. I talked that way thinking of the time of the king. Today, we're in another world, the police are hard at work for the people, they even do the work of judges and lawyers. Do what you feel like doing. The important thing is that Azad, Shero Selim Malay's son, obtain a university diploma." He stopped, looked me straight in the eye, and added, "Promise?" "I promise," I answered.

I was entering the years of awakening: painting, books, my math teacher, Sartre, George Bernard Shaw, everything was helping me grow out of childhood. I made new friends: Jemal, Ako, Imad . . . Jemal was a student in the technical school of agronomy, Ako was in the teachers' training college, and Imad was the musician of our group. He played the lute and the violin extremely well. We liked to get together at Ako's—especially me, because his sister Nazik was fond of me. She was a small brunette full of vitality, with black eyes and long hair. Whenever I left her house, she would slip love letters into my jacket, and as a way of winning me over, she would mix references to Kurdistan and patriotism with words describing my "beauty" and her love for me. Sitting in a room, we would liberate Kurdistan and give power to the working class. Jemal, the son of Abdulla the Communist barber, would talk to us, in no logical order, about the glory of Stalin, Ceauşescu, and Brezhnev, the genius of Erich Honecker, the courage of Enver Hoxha, the technological progress of the Eastern bloc countries. "But why are all these great men friends of Saddam?" Jemal's reply to me was, "Your father listens to Voice of America too much." At that point Imad would take out his lute and we'd start singing, and Nazik, under the pretext of serving tea, would walk by me several times, throwing me ardent glances.

My friends were several years older than I. They wore sideburns, but I didn't have enough of a beard to grow mine. So I colored them in with my mother's kohl.

On Thursdays and Fridays we would spend the evenings in a bar owned by Armenians. We would drink raki with our meze, and the waiters thought we were artists. One evening, I saw Sami the painter come in. He greeted us and went to sit in a corner. We didn't dare invite him to our table, knowing that he liked to be alone. He ordered some raki and lit a cigarette. I was glad to be frequenting the same bar as he. My friends and I were once again remaking the world—and drinking, too. There was no one in the bar but Sami and us, and even though we were having a lively conversation, the waiters didn't seem to be paying attention to what we were saying. To my great surprise, Sami called out to us, "We Kurds will never amount to anything. We are cursed, that is our destiny. Look at our history, we're the most ancient people in the region, and yet the Turks, who came after us, have their own state, and we have nothing." Finger pointing to his temple, he added, "But the strangest thing is that in spite of the massacres, we're still here. The Chaldeans, the Babylonians, the Sumerians built empires and nothing is left of them. As for us, we're still here, speaking our language, and yet unable to make anything of ourselves. We refuse to be subjugated, we rebel, and we're still nothing . . ." Imad turned to Sami, smiling. "What you're saying is contradictory." "You can't speak," replied Sami calmly, "you signed up." Imad turned pale; he was speechless. Signing up meant joining the Baath Party. How else could he have been accepted into a school as politically sensitive as the Baghdad Music Conservatory?

The evening ended without incident. We, his friends, knew Imad had signed up only because of his passion for music. And being seen with him, a party member, was a good cover for our group. But the security forces knew how to manipulate us and sow the seeds of doubt in each of us. We all suspected each other, friends, brothers . . . But as one of our proverbs says, "The mouth is not a hole in a wall that can be filled in with mud."

For July 17, the anniversary of the Baathist Party's coming to power, loudspeakers were set up around the town hall on Aqra's main square. The walls were decorated with slogans and photos of the president. The local Baath Party leader was going to speak, and students, government employees, everyone had to attend. I was present when the party leader began his speech with greetings to the president. Half the people assembled on the square belonged to the security forces; they began applauding and we followed suit. Someone cried out, "Long live the president!" and we all chimed in, "Long live the knight of the Arab nation!" Everyone cried out in unison. The speaker resumed his speech. Quiet had returned when someone in the crowd began to shout, "Long live General Barzani! Long live Kurdistan!" The scattered security officers immediately converged on the spot where this shout had originated. It was Sami the painter. He had stripped off his clothes as a sign of protest. We saw the policemen grab him like a wisp of straw while Sami continued to shout, "Long live freedom! Long live Kurdistan!" I never saw Sami again, nor his paintings of Kurdish women nor his portraits of the general.

I was told that he spent his time writing letters to Kurt Waldheim, Jimmy Carter, Giscard d'Estaing, asking that they assist the Kurds.

One day I was summoned by the headmaster during math class. Jacob, my teacher, looked slightly worried as he gave me leave. I followed the caretaker up the long hallway to the headmaster's office, but before I reached the door, the caretaker signaled to me to enter the neighboring office, the one with the "Do Not Enter" sign. I knocked and walked in. The man with the drooping mustache was waiting for me, but he wasn't alone. Two other men from the security forces were present. Strangely, I was no longer afraid. This wasn't the first time I'd been summoned. I wasn't trembling; I already pictured myself a martyr. Immediately the man with the mustache asked me if I had enrolled in the Baathist Youth. "Sir, the only thing I care about in life is painting," I replied. "My dream is to study art in Europe. After that, I'll be worthy of joining the party."

"Bravo," he said, "the party will help you. You have the choice: either sign up and the party sends you to Europe, or don't sign up and the party sees to it that you disappear." The two other men rose, impatient, and my interlocutor told me to follow them out. "They have things to see you about." I followed calmly in their footsteps. They made me climb into a white Land Cruiser parked in front of the school, and I sat squeezed between the two of them. They took me directly to the security offices opposite the hospital. There they asked one of their colleagues whether they should bring me to the basement. I started to become truly frightened; I knew, as everyone did, that the basement was where they tortured and executed people. Finally, they led me into a small room on the ground floor, with no window or light, and locked the door. A half hour later, the door opened and I was pulled into the office of the head security officer. He had a tape recorder on his desk, and he started questioning me about my brother the fighter. "I know nothing at all about him." He showered me with questions. "What about his friends, what do they say? What do they know?" "I don't know them, they're too old for me." "Why didn't you report him when he joined the fighters?" "Among us, a younger brother doesn't have the right to ask his older brother anything!" "Fine, that's true . . . We're kind to decent people. I'll let you go, but come back to see me regularly, whenever you have something to tell me." The session had lasted about forty minutes. I left his office and found myself at the door of the security building, blushing with shame—and worried, for if someone should come down the street at that moment and see me leaving un-harmed, they would assume I was a collaborator.

I walked down the street, head lowered, glancing furtively around to see if any acquaintances were passing by. Fortu-nately, there was no one, and I ran off as fast as I could. Only when I was some distance away did I begin to think about the questions the head of security had asked me. I was deal-ing with an intelligent man who believed he could use me as an informer by employing gentle methods.

All the librarians had received a list of books that had to be sent to Baghdad to be destroyed. These were old books whose flaw was that they didn't follow the Baathist line. Be-cause he trusted me, our town librarian had given me some Kurdish books, and I considered it my patriotic duty to hide them for safekeeping.

I was prepared to do anything for the Kurdish cause. I wanted to make movies, but I knew that I had no chance of being admitted to the film institute: the school was for Baathists exclusively, and advantage was given to Arabs. I wanted to skip ahead, catch up in school, and make up for lost time. I was eager to become a man, and to be more bril-liant and courageous than my friends. I wanted to be a hero and come up with new fighting methods for my people. And I felt my time had come. I spent days in endless palaver with my friends, my head brimming with ideas, but I was disappointed in my pals, who weren't active enough. I be-came solitary.

Up in my room, on the second floor, I mulled these things over, including the fact that the secret police were at my heels. I had to make a decision.

My cousin Ramo dropped by to see me, well dressed and very perfumed, his sparse beard clean-shaven. He wanted us to go for a walk downtown, and invited me for lunch at his parents' house afterward. But that day I had come to a decision and had other plans in my head. I went downstairs and saw my mother, in her black dress, busy with the housework; I watched her for a long time as a way of saying goodbye. She said to me, simply, "Don't come home late, and be careful." I smiled at her to put her mind at rest. "*Dayé*, Mother, don't worry, your son isn't a kid anymore." I was dying to kiss her, but I was afraid of revealing my plan, and feared she might cry and stir up the whole neighborhood.

I left the house with two cents in my pocket and headed straight for the bus station. Ramo, who very much wanted me to regard him as a courageous person, followed me. "Where are we going?" "How much do you have on you?" He rummaged through his pockets, "Twelve dinars, why?" "We're going to join the partisans." "What? We're going to the mountains? Why didn't you warn me so I could be prepared?" "Real men must always be prepared." I was a person of conviction. I added, "But if you don't want to come . . ." Full of pride, he cut me off immediately, "The Kurds have a saying, *Kem bijî, kel bijî.*★ Come on, let's go!"

At the station, we got into an old shared cab and drove off. We had to cross about a dozen checkpoints and show our student identification papers. I had a contact in the village of Harin. When the cab dropped us off, we continued on foot toward the mountains.

We arrived in Harin at sunset. We were welcomed by roving dogs that barked when they saw us trying stealthily to

★Literally, "Live little, live hot." —Translator's note

find our way. I located Saïd's house; he was the contact who was going to help us join the partisans. I knocked on the window. He was sitting with his wife and baby, drinking tea in the one room of the house. He opened the door and welcomed us warmly. He was my sister-in-law Dijla's brother-in-law. In a few words, I told him we wanted to join the fighters. He turned to his wife and asked her to serve us tea, then he went out, telling us to wait for him. We were left alone with his wife, who was very shy, and the baby, who was poking his finger at a partridge huddled in a cage. The baby went around the cage trying by every means to touch the bird. Each time he managed to do so, the bird would let out a plaintive cry and peck him, but this didn't dissuade the little boy, who continued his game. The partridge hopped up and down to escape his young torturer, but when his head hit the top of the cage, the child poked him in the head. His mother sat silently in front of the teapot. Every once in a while, she pulled the child toward her, but as soon as she let him go, he went back to the cage. The baby carried on like this the entire time we waited for his father. Saïd finally returned and motioned for us to leave. Ramo and I would gladly have spent the night at Saïd's, but he didn't have the courage to make such an offer. Before parting from us, he filled our pockets with raisins.

Saïd pointed to a road leading out of the village about a hundred yards from his house, and told us that someone was waiting for us a half mile from there. "He's your guide. When you see him, say 'Tetras.' He should answer 'Lion.'" We left the village cautiously. "What if Saïd is an informer?" It was a pitch-black night and we saw the glow of a cigarette. A man approached us. We cried out, "Tetras." We were blinded by a beam of light that swept up and down over us. Then we heard a loud roar of laughter. I repeated "Tetras"; still no answer, just laughter. So I yelled "Tetras" curtly. He finally answered "Lion."

"Hey, townsfolk, where are you going in your elegant clothes—to a wedding?" I was wearing denim trousers and a matching shirt with an embroidered rose on the front. "We didn't want to attract the attention of the policemen at the checkpoints . . ." In spite of our explanation, he went on laughing. We were beginning to fade from exhaustion, but we followed him, as he went prancing like a gazelle about fifty yards ahead of us. He'd turn around, wait for us to catch up, and laugh again at the sight of us. His welcome greatly disappointed me, but I said nothing. Soon we had covered quite a distance, and all we could think about was stopping to rest for a few minutes, but he completely disregarded our fatigue. At sunrise we reached a small hamlet. He made us go into a house while he remained on the doorstep whispering with the owner. After five minutes, our guide poked his head through the half-open door and said, "My mission is accomplished; now he'll take care of you," and he left. Our new guide introduced himself; his name was Khidir. While he was making breakfast, we dozed off for an hour.

As we walked in the mountains, I noticed that a bird had been flying above us for some time. It would land about a hundred meters away and wait until we reached that point, then fly off and land a bit farther on. The bird's song was sorrowful. Very pleased with this new companion, Khidir followed the flight of the bird attentively, and spoke to us about the struggle for Kurdish independence with an optimism that reminded me of my father's, years earlier. He could talk forever, praising the courage and political genius of the fighters we were joining, while the bird went with us every step of the way. Then Khidir began telling us the story of the bird. "In the age of Solomon, two sisters lost sight of each other. In their search for one another, they changed into birds and flew all over the sky . . ." Ever since, it has been said that the bird flying over us is one of the sisters, eternally seeking her sibling. He spoke of the grief of the two sisters changed into birds, and deeply believed in his story. As I watched him, I was overcome by pity. How could a people so naïve ever liberate themselves in the days of Henry Kissinger and Andrei Gromyko, the most cynical politicians of the century? The bird triggered something in my mind. Suddenly I no longer believed in our fighting methods.

I continued to follow Khidir. He was a good man, dependable and very attentive. As soon as he would see us slow our pace, he'd find a pretext for stopping. "Brothers, I'm a little tired, let's take a rest." He'd dig in his pocket and take out some dried figs, walnuts, or a piece of bread, which we would share. He took us to the top of Mount Gara. Then he told us to wait. He disappeared for a short time and reappeared with three fighters with Kalashnikovs on their shoulders. He embraced us and, by way of farewell, expressed the wish to see us again, the next time in a free country. Then he made his way back through the mountains to return to his family. The fighters greeted us; one of them made tea, another stood guard; and they all took some bread out of their bags. We ate, the Kalashnikovs on the ground next to us. The leader didn't say a word to us. At nightfall, he asked me my name. I told him I was Azad, son of Shero, the general's personal operator, but his expression didn't change.

We spent a week with them, walking with no apparent goal. Due to fatigue, hunger, and cold, Ramo could no longer think straight. As for me, I thought we should bear with them a bit longer, to give them a chance to get to know us better. Then, perhaps, they would tell us their plans. It was natural for them not to trust us immediately. During a rest period, as the leader drank his tea, he told me he knew who I was. Angry, I asked him to give me a weapon and fighter's clothes and send me out on an opera-tion. He told me we were going to be sent to another region where men were needed. I wanted to leave at once, but he replied, "In a week."

At every stopping place, someone was elected to stand guard. My turn came. A fighter was ordered to lend me his weapon. He handed me his Kalashnikov and I went to the designated site. Leaning against a rock, I looked out over the vast landscape and surmised that the black spots in the valleys were destroyed villages. I aimed my weapon all around me, feeling like a true Napoleon. I wished the entire Iraqi army would show up so I could take it on single-handed. And then I recalled my father's old Brno. What had we gained from all those years of struggle? Something else was needed, but what? I had no answer. I looked at the Kalashnikov, and it seemed clearer and clearer to me that we couldn't dig a tunnel with a needle. I began to weep over our fate. And then I heard footfalls. Two hours had gone by. I wiped my eyes; someone was coming to relieve me.

Two weeks went by and the leader still said nothing about transferring us to another group. Finally, he asked both of us to come talk to him alone. We sat under a tree and he drew a circle on the ground, which he divided into four sections: in the north, Turkey; and the south, Iraq; in the west, Syria, and the east, Iran. "This is our homeland. You're students; our people need educated persons, and they also need fighters in the towns. If you're courageous, return to your town, go back to your studies, and help us organize acts of sabotage." Then he spent several days teaching us how to handle explosives and weapons. Someone would contact us when we returned.

The group of fighters escorted us to the last village before the Iraqi lines. We were given five dinars each. I was worried: how were we going to get back into the zone controlled by the Iraqis? It wouldn't be so easy. Before we parted, the leader said only, "Comrade, life is a risk; being born is a risk." He took leave of us, and we saw him go back into the mountains with his men. A peasant was supposed to help us cross the Iraqi lines.

We were ready to leave before dawn, but the peasant told us it was too early. I knew the Iraqi army came to the villages at dawn and combed through them and I didn't want to dawdle. I insisted, but the man remained indifferent. I wondered if we weren't in the hands of a collaborator and if he wasn't playing a double game with the fighters. Ramo and I went outside the house to avoid the risk of being surrounded. Finally our host followed us, slipping a pistol into his belt, and we set off. He showed us the bridge guarded by Iraqi soldiers that we had to cross. "May luck be with you," he said, and made an about-face. We walked down to the bridge with our prepared answers: we were volunteers for the literacy campaign. We approached the soldiers; I greeted them with a resounding "hello" and a smile, and they answered in kind. More soldiers were at the other end of the bridge. I avoided looking at Ramo, who was deathly pale. I wondered if they hadn't let us pass in order to trap us in the middle of the bridge between the two checkpoints. We were still wearing our city clothes, but we were visibly filthy and gave off a strong odor. We reached the second checkpoint and greeted them; no one asked us anything, and then we were on the main road. Our sangfroid had prevailed. I became convinced they had taken us for informers. Relieved, I said to Ramo, "The sun protected us, Zarathustra is on our side." We hailed a shared cab. There was only one free seat, but the driver accepted both of us. Ramo climbed in front, and I climbed in the rear, next to a fat, well-dressed man with a cigarette between his fingers, who was sprawled out, squeezing me into a corner. I tried to make myself tiny, but he kept crushing me. I looked at him, annoyed, and pushed back a little. He glared at me and cramped me even more. I said, "May the devil be damned," and he retorted, "May the infidels be damned." It was a real squabble, with us locking horns in the rear of the cab, and then we came to an abrupt stop: an Iraqi army commando was pointing weapons at our car. I was prepared for anything. The officer leaned in the window and asked for the passengers' papers. Just as Ramo was about to be checked, my fat neighbor raised his hand and greeted the officer. The officer bent down and responded in kind, then gave us the go-ahead. My neighbor was a pro-government Kurdish militiaman who was known to the military. I stopped giving him the evil eye, and even conceded a bit more space: in spite of himself, he had become my protector, my *laissez-passer*. He looked at me and I responded with a broad smile, even though deep down I wanted to kill him. To my surprise, he smiled back, and I realized he assumed I was a collaborator! Fortunately we didn't exchange a word. And thanks to him we got through every checkpoint all the way to the first big town, Amadiyeh, and never once were our papers checked. We had to change cars; I hoped that our neighbor would continue on with us, but he had reached the end of his trip.

It was a Friday and the cab station was overrun with soldiers on leave. As soon as a car drove up, they would take it by storm. We couldn't compete with them; they had priority. Then a cab drove up and parked in an isolated part of the station. The soldiers threw themselves on it, but the driver stepped out and declared that his car had broken down. I watched him as he went to drink some tea and had a feeling he was deceiving the soldiers. I went up to him and asked him if he could take us to Dihok. "My car broke down." "How much do you want?" He asked for double the normal price. I went to ask the few civilians at the station if they would agree to pay double the price. If not, we would remain stranded in this town full of soldiers. I succeeded in convincing three of them. Then we had to solve a major problem: how were we ever going to take this cab away right under the soldiers' noses? I told the driver to drive off from the station and to wait for us in a specific spot in town; we would walk to meet him there.

I no longer had a cent in my pocket. In the cab I sat next to an older man who seemed well off. He kept looking at my wristwatch. He wanted to buy it, but I explained that it was a very cherished gift and I couldn't part with it. Ramo was shoving me, but I signaled him to keep quiet. We were approaching Dihok and the driver began asking each of us for our fares. As usual, someone had to be in charge of collecting the money. I volunteered and handed the money to the driver. While driving, he glanced down at the bills, and pointed out that two fares were missing. "That's true," I replied, unperturbed, "it's my friend and me. We don't have any money." He almost lost control of the car, and the passengers raised their arms in alarm. "What?" yelled the driver. "You arranged everything, you agreed to pay double the price, and now you're telling me you can't pay!" "There are two possible solutions," I said calmly. "Either you drop us off at the side of the road, or you understand that we have to get to Dihok and you'll be nice to us." The driver fell silent; we were getting to town and he really had no choice. In any case, he was getting off lightly since three out of five passengers were paying double the fare. When we arrived, I thanked him, and then caught up with the elderly gentleman who wanted to buy my watch. "I agree to sell you my watch. It's difficult for me to part with it, but as you may have noticed, we don't have a single dinar." After bargaining briefly, I sold him my cheap watch for a good price. And for the first time, I felt truly dishonest.

Pocketing the money, Ramo and I ran to a restaurant. Like two famished wolves, each of us devoured a chicken, bread, onions, parsley, and cucumbers, and washed it all down with several beers. We had spent hardly a quarter of our fortune. In the afternoon, we left for Mosul, where my friend's sister lived. For the first time in twenty days, we plunged into delightful baths, and in the evening we went to see an Indian movie at the Semiramis.

When we got home, Ramo's sister greeted us very angrily. She saw me as having compromised her brother. We decided to part and return to Aqra separately, not knowing what was lying in store for us. I didn't see him again for a while; his family wouldn't allow him to see the person responsible for our escapade.

Other friends started to avoid me. I knew that some among them now held me in higher esteem, but I represented a danger. I was still free to do as I pleased, though the security forces knew of my activities; they were letting the fruit ripen, waiting to see whom I came into contact with so they could haul us all in. From the fighters there was dead silence; no one brought me explosives or weapons. I spent most of my time at home reading and painting, and I watched my father become increasingly despondent; he would get irritated over nothing, brood despairingly, and isolate himself more and more often. Looking out the window, I watched him walk around the orchard, stop, gaze at the pomegranate trees, and walk back toward the house when my mother called him, hands behind his back, hunched over, looking shattered.

Zilan, my little niece, fell sick. Her whole body was swollen. Two days earlier, during singing class, instead of singing the song to the glory of the president and the Baath Party, she had intoned a patriotic Kurdish song. The schoolmistress, a Baathist, dragged her to the headmaster's office and quizzed her to find out who had taught her the song and what she and her family thought of the president and the Iraqis. Zilan felt guilty. She realized she had made a mistake, and we advised her never to do it again. The better to persuade her, we said to her, "You could endanger your father's life if you sing that kind of song." And following that incident, she fell sick. Sitting in the garden, my father called out to her; she came out, pale, and threw herself in his arms. Zilan was our little favorite, and my father wanted to put her mind at ease. "My girl, don't worry for your father, he's safe in the mountains, and the Iraqis can't hurt him." He asked me to take her to the hospital, as he was too tired to go. I took Zilan in my arms and we set off. Along the way, we stopped to drink some Coca-Cola; she wanted to walk, and we continued on foot.

In the hospital, the nurse, who was addressed as "Doctor," hardly examined her, and then gave me tablets wrapped in newspaper. Upon returning home, I resumed painting. Zilan lay on a mattress next to me, wrapped in a blanket. I was very fond of her, and when I told her I wanted to paint her portrait, she threw off the blanket and stood up happily.

Jacob, my math teacher, wanted to see me. To avoid attracting attention, we agreed to meet in an Arab café in Mosul, seventy kilometers away. When I arrived, Jacob was reading *Al Saoura*, the Baathist newspaper, and on the table in front of him was a cup of tea swarming with flies. We went out and walked toward Bab el-Tob, the noisiest working-class neighborhood in the city. While walking, lost in the crowd, we could safely talk. I no longer thought much about the revolution and its old methods; I wanted to move on to something else. I returned to Aqra at nightfall. Zilan had become more seriously ill and my father was tucking in her blankets. When he saw me, he begged me, with tearful eyes, to go back to the hospital with her. He was worn out. I smiled at him. "Papa, I couldn't have imagined that Shero, the general's personal operator, could be so demoralized." He said only, "That time is over, my boy, it's all done in." I bent down and kissed Zilan. A wheeze rose up in her tiny chest; she was breathing with difficulty, and her condition was worsening. I took her in my arms, wrapped her in a blanket, and headed back to the hospital. She was trying desperately to breathe. I kissed her to reassure her, and quickened my pace, taking a shortcut that ran in front of the Baath Party offices, a dangerous street at night because they were known to shoot on sight. More and more she seemed to be suffocating. When we finally arrived at the hospital, I put her down on a bed in an empty room and asked the nurse to call a physician immediately. He ran out, and I returned to Zilan's bedside. I was beside myself. I kept kissing her, saying, "Everything's fine, the doctor is coming." The nurse returned without the physician and I sent him away again, insisting that a doctor come at once. I went back to my niece's bedside and watched over her breathing, fearing it might stop. Minutes went by, interminable minutes, and still there was no doctor. I couldn't bear it anymore: I ran down the corridor to the door of the physician's office and banged on it, to no effect. Returning again to Zilan's bedside, I saw a vague glimmer of light in her eyes, but the doctor still didn't come. I went back to his door and hammered away on it, and finally he opened it. He was combing his hair. We had already seen each other at the headquarters of the secret police. He gave me a nasty look before walking slowly down the corridor. I ran ahead of him. When he came into Zilan's room, I cried, "She's stopped breathing!" Impassively, the doctor asked, "She's the terrorist's daughter?" "She's a child, that's all. Do something!" He started yelling, "You monkey, you think you can order me around?" I implored him. He signaled to the nurse to bring oxygen bottles. I helped him carry them; they were very light and I thought they might be empty. I looked at both of them. "They're empty . . ." The doctor ignored my remark. I no longer knew what to do. I saw him place the mask on

Zilan's face. I saw her move her head slightly, and two minutes later the doctor removed the mask. "It's over," he said curtly to the nurse, and walked out. I looked at Zilan and felt all my energy drain out of me. I broke down over the body of my niece. Then I stood up and went out. I was calm, but I began to cough up blood. The nurse returned Zilan's body to my father, wrapped in a white sheet, in the back of a pickup truck.

I was of age, even if I was only fourteen on paper. People knew me as a calm but dangerous boy; my friends saw me as mysterious, the government agents as a mosquito, and my mother as a dog with scalded paws who couldn't stand still. As for me, I saw myself as a combination of all these.

"Calm down a bit, my son," my mother would repeat all day long. But nothing could calm me. I had been neglecting my studies for quite a while; I spent much of my time in my room on the second floor. Soon it was spring, and the pomegranate trees were in bloom—I could see them from my window. I gazed out at them, gazed at the early spring light, and gazed down at the book in front of me on my table. I heard the sound of my mother's footsteps as she climbed upstairs. She checked on me when she could. "What are you doing, my son?" she asked. "As you can see, Mama, I'm studying." My mother leaned over the table and shut the book. She looked at the cover and the first few pages, then looked at me. "My son, why do you mock me? Telling me you're studying!" "Well, Mama, isn't this a book here in front of me?" I joked. "My son, I'm talking about schoolbooks!"

My mother couldn't read well, and she read even less well

in Arabic, but she knew which books were schoolbooks and which ones weren't, for the schoolbooks all had a photo of Saddam Hussein on the cover, smoking a cigar, shooting a pistol, or hunting on horseback in traditional Arab dress, sporting a Kalashnikov . . . She felt duped, and turned to leave. I saw her small figure in her black jacket, silhouetted in the door, and then I listened to her go down the stairs. I stood up, went to the window, and stared outside. In my mind, I was planning my escape, perhaps to Europe.

I left the house, and I heard my mother cry out to me, "My son, don't come home late." I ran into my cousin Ramo, and we went to a pub and ordered a half bottle of arak. The Assyrian waiter brought us the half bottle with the customary bowl of chickpeas as meze. Ramo was all ears. "I'm leaving, maybe for Europe," I said, looking him straight in the eye. He smiled. "I'd like to go too," he said, "but I'm a year away from my diploma. Wait for me and we'll go together." I smiled back. Ramo thought I had no future in my studies, whereas he did. He was already branded from having followed me into the mountains, and he didn't want to make the same mistake twice. "Even if everyone could leave Iraq," he said to me, "you'd never stand a chance. First of all, you have to be a Baathist, and even then, trips are forbidden." We stopped speaking when two men came in and sat down at a table. One of the two was Kamal. He looked at me. In Aqra everyone knew everyone, but I knew Kamal especially well. He was one of my brother Dilovan's childhood friends, but for the last three years my brother had refused to speak to him, apart from curt hellos: Kamal had become not only a Baathist but a party official. Kamal kept turning to look at me, but this didn't surprise me because I knew I was suspect. I finished my glass of arak and we left the bar.

The next day, I was waiting for my friend Ako in the tea-room in the Saraï Bazaar. The tearoom was full of people; old people and the unemployed played dominoes, smoked tobacco, and spat on the floor. The steam from the samovar made the air heavy. Outside it was drizzling; it was the last cold spell of the season. The big portrait of Saddam Hussein hanging on the glass door made it difficult for me to see outside. The waiter brought me some tea. Through the glass door, I watched Kamal go by, and he saw me. Every time a car drove past, it spattered mud on the glass and on Saddam Hussein's portrait, so the owner gave the waiter a rag so he could clean off the mud right away, which he did. This wasn't a matter of cleanliness or aesthetics, but because it was really dangerous to neglect the president's portrait. Gradually it stopped raining, but there was still enough mud in the street to spatter the portrait. After a while the waiter stopped serving tea and remained posted by the door with his cleaning rag. I saw Kamal walk by the tearoom again and look in at me; he was dripping wet. I felt like standing up and leaving, or like grabbing him by the collar and asking him what he wanted. I went to the door and saw him standing a short way off, motionless, smoking a cigarette. We exchanged looks. I knew I was being tailed, but I couldn't have imagined it would be by Kamal, a Kurd and one of my brother's old pals. I went back and sat down again; I had to wait for Ako, who was already very late. The waiter continued to clean the glass. He spit on a few stubborn drops of automobile grease and wiped them with his rag. I was delighted to see him spit on the portrait. In a flash, the owner left his samovar, pounced on him, grabbed him by the ear, and pulled him to the far end of the room. He smacked him hard in the face. "If someone had seen you, you little ass, my tearoom would have been razed to the ground." I watched, unable to intervene. Even with the smack, I felt the boy was still the winner!

Suddenly Kamal reappeared in front of the window and signaled me to come out. I went out to him. I wasn't afraid. "What's up?" "Come along." I followed him; he walked a few steps ahead of me; he didn't want people to see us to-gether lest they suspect him. Nor did I, for the same reason. He stopped in an isolated spot, glanced around, and said, "You're Dilovan's brother, and I wish you both well. I know you're about to be arrested; I saw your file at party head-quarters. I felt I should warn you before they arrest you." I listened to him in astonishment, and he continued, "You see, I don't cause anyone harm." "But you're not just a party member," I said, "you're an official." "I'm a ghost official, they don't trust me. I'm a Kurd! It's just that I have to pro-tect my family . . . I've told you, you must find a solution! If you hear from your brother, send him my greetings . . ."

Kamal left; I remained on the spot. I was a little fright-ened and wondered if I should run away immediately. But I was supposed to see Ako. I went back to the tearoom, suspi-cious of every person who crossed my path. Inside Jemal, the son of Abdulla the Communist barber, was waiting for me, looking preoccupied.

"Where's Ako?" I asked. "Ako is having problems; his sis-ter Nazik has run away with a man." This made me forget Kamal and all my worries. Nazik was the girl who slipped love letters into my jacket pocket whenever I went over to see Ako. "Nazik . . . she ran away? With a man . . . ?"

I went home and reread her letters. "My dear Azad, you are the love of my heart . . ." But I wasn't really very sad; the only woman for me, the love of my life, was Jian, the girl who had given me a flashlight.

On the radio, on the television, and in the state newspapers, we started hearing about Hafiz al-Assad's great wisdom, his rapprochement with Saddam Hussein, and an impending union between Syria and Iraq. I couldn't believe my eyes or ears, even though I knew he was a despotic president and his state a Baathist state, because up until then Assad had been described as a traitor to the Arab nation.

The party organized celebrations everywhere in Iraq, even in Aqra. Everyone talked of the two presidents. Saddam Hussein had merely to say the moon shines during the day and the sun at night, and everyone became blind. With the first signs of unity between the two Baathist countries, movement opened up on both sides of the Syrian-Iraqi frontier, and euphoria set in. Now I was happy at last, for Arab unity was providing me with the chance of a lifetime! For ages I'd been trying to think of a way to get a passport so I could flee Iraq, and during this period all the administrative offices, the police, and the secret police were taken up with the celebrations. I went to the passport office in Mosul and submitted my application. The officer of the secret police glanced at it; my age was the only problem. Officially I was fourteen and had to be accompanied. "I am going with my guardian; he has agreed to this because the Iraqi Baathist Youth is paying a visit to our brothers, the Syrian Baathist Youth. I would hate to fail in my patriotic duty." The officer looked at me. "Come back with a party certificate and your guardian."

For the first time in my life, I took a taxi alone. I went straight to the restaurant owned by a relative of ours in Mosul. I lied to him, saying that my family has asked him if he'd become my guardian. The man was about sixty, had a pleasant appearance, and above all spoke perfect Arabic. He climbed into the taxi with me, but after a few minutes asked the driver to stop and whispered in my ear: "If you've become a Baath Party member, I won't help you." I said: "You know everyone in my family, how could you think we would sell out?" After a moment of reflection, he said to me, "No, I don't . . . Forgive me. But we live in a time when a father can no longer trust his son. Fine, let's go."

We arrived at the headquarters of the secret police, the *mokhabarat*. I had remembered to buy the Party newspaper, *Al Saoura*, and I slipped it conspicuously under my arm, but I had no party certificate. The officer took a hard look at the man who was with me. "You consent?" "Of course; the students are leaving for the celebration of Arab unity!" The officer made my guardian sign a paper, and that's all he asked for, forgetting the certificate. "You can come back for your passport at 4 p.m."

At four o'clock sharp, I held a passport in my hand, and felt deliriously happy. I leafed through it; a red stamp stated TRAVEL TO ISRAEL PROHIBITED. I didn't care, I didn't plan to go there. I turned the page and saw another stamp, TRAVEL PROHIBITED WITHOUT A GUARDIAN. This alarmed me, as everything was untrue: the purpose of the trip, the guardian . . . But I had a passport in my pocket! I strolled around Mosul's dirty streets and imagined myself in Europe, an important man, holding hands with a blonde like the Russian woman in Billē and doing things for the Kurds . . .

I spent several days at home, scrutinizing my parents' faces. I also gazed at the trees in our orchard, gazed at my town, at the streets, at my pals. I was no longer the same person. My family had suspicions about my imminent departure, but I said nothing. "My son, I see conspiracies in your eyes," my mother said to me. I smiled. "Mama, your son's eyes are the eyes of a man." Then I asked, "Mama, you like knowing your son is alive, don't you?" "Oh, you're ruthless, how can you doubt a mother's heart!" She was melancholy. "Fine, my son, fine . . . The important thing is for you to be alive, and that no misfortune befall you . . ."

Given the nature of this separation and the distance involved, I knew I might never see my parents alive again. It was obvious that as long as the Baath Party was in power, there'd be no hope of our finding each other in the future. If I had told them outright that I was going into exile, they wouldn't have stopped me, but to them I was still a kid, their kid. They couldn't have endured the pain of parting and saying farewell. Who can bear to see tears flowing? But in this country everything was uncertain, everything was ephemeral.

The opportunity presented itself at the wedding of my cousin Galavej. She was Cheto's sister, Cheto of the stunt pigeons, and the wedding was to take place in another town, Erbil. We were all invited. My mother was very fond of her brother's children. On that Thursday morning, for the first time in years, I saw her forgo her black outfit and take out a dark red dress with tiny blue flowers: she was happy. So was I, at the sight of her happiness. My father put on his new Kurdish suit. My mother darkened her eyes with kohl; the white, cloudlike spot in the middle of her iris was visible, but she was beautiful and happy.

In my room, I packed a small traveling bag. I put in a Kurdish suit, a cassette of Kurdish music, and a book of Kurdish poetry and went downstairs. "Are you ready?" my parents said in unison. I could feel my heart pounding wildly and tears coming to my eyes. I was afraid this was the last time I'd see them. I had no idea what the future held. I went on looking at them, both so happy. I leaned toward my mother and picked her up in my arms like a bride, lifted her, and kissed her. She laughed, and so did my father. I continued kissing her for a moment, breathing in her odor, as she had with my brother when he returned from the mountains after all those years. Calmly and gently, I set her down and went to kiss my father. He laughed. "Why are you kissing me? I'm not going away." "Does a son have to have a special reason to kiss his father?" "Of course not, my son, come here," he said, and pulled me close and kissed me. It was difficult for me. I felt like crying, but it was better to part this way. "You're leaving before we do?" asked my father. I didn't answer. I looked at him. "Papa, you should know

your son is proud of his father, the general's personal operator . . ." I left them, with pangs of anguish, and walked
down the street. I couldn't bring myself to turn around.

I climbed into a car heading straight for the Turkish frontier;
it was inconceivable to go to Baathist Syria, I thought. Six
hours later I was at the border between Iraq and Turkey. After a great many checkpoints, I finally reached the last one,
the checkpoint of the secret police. There were no travelers;
it was strictly a trade route. A security officer asked me for
my papers. I handed him my passport. "Where are you planning to go?" he asked me with a mocking smile. He was
face to face with a kid. "To Turkey, for a week of tourism."
"During the school term?" "I've been given permission."
He shut the passport and spoke to me as to a child: "If
you're giving me lip, I hear you." "I don't understand what
you're saying; the government gave me this passport," I
replied fearlessly. The officer called a soldier over and turned
back to me, dead serious. "I don't want you turning up at
the frontier ever again. If you do, you're dead." He handed
me my passport and asked the soldier to take me back to the
car station. I climbed into the security jeep, preparing myself
for the worst. I didn't think he'd take me to the station. We
set off but, after eight checkpoints, to my surprise the man
dropped me off at the station without a word.

My first attempt had failed, but I was relieved. The wolves
hadn't devoured me yet. Wasting no time, I took the road to
Mosul; from there cars left for Syria. Two and a half hours
later I was at the Mosul station, trying to find a car to Syria.
I saw my cousin Cheto, who was a student at Mosul University. He had spruced himself up and was going to his sister's wedding, like my mother and father. We greeted each
other; he assumed I was also going to the wedding. "Go

ahead, I'll be coming soon," I said to him. He was already at university, whereas I hadn't even finished school. To him, I was a failure, a reckless and undisciplined person. He looked at me and left. I resumed my search for a car to take me to the border. A driver standing next to an old station wagon was crying out, "Syria! Syria!" I signaled to him and got into the back of the car. Three Arab villagers climbed in as well, with their bags and baskets. There was some space left next to the driver for a young boy who said a few words to him in Kurdish. I understood they were Kurds from Syria. This made me happy, but I said nothing. I didn't want anyone to know anything about me.

The car drove out of Mosul in the direction of the frontier. At five in the morning we arrived at Rabia, on the Iraq-Syria border. We were the only car in the desert. We stopped in front of a tiny checkpoint, and I became anxious. A soldier with a Kalashnikov collected all the passengers' passports and went into the checkpoint office. I made myself inconspicuous and tried to calm my nerves with the thoughts that the place didn't look like a border checkpoint and that the young soldier looked pitiful. I waited. The driver got out and went to pee behind a wall. The soldier returned and handed papers to everyone except me. He made me step out and follow him. I obeyed, very worried. Inside the checkpoint office, I saw a fat, swarthy man with a drooping mustache and sleepy eyes. "What are you doing here?" he asked me. "I'd like—" "Shut up, you piece of dog shit." He ordered the soldier to lock me in a cagelike cell— me, the piece of dog shit—so he could show me a wild time later, after he'd woken up. And he told the soldier to warn the secret police. Then he took my passport and went into his room.

I was alone with the young soldier, who was getting ready to put me in the cell. I asked him to let me go outside to pay the driver my fare. He consented and walked me back to the car. All the passengers were waiting for me, calm and discreet. I stuck my head through the car window and put my mouth close to the driver's ear. "I can't continue, they've arrested me," I said in Kurdish. The driver's mouth gaped open. "You're a Kurd?" he said. "Yes," I answered, with a bitter smile. He swooped out of the car like an eagle, signaled me to stay put, and asked the soldier to follow him. They went into the office. Ten minutes later the driver came out, alone, with my passport in his hands. "Get in, we're off," he said. My heart soared with joy.

The driver made me change places with an Arab sitting in the front, and placed me between himself and the other young Kurdish boy. The car crossed the border. I could not believe my eyes. The driver looked at me, smiling. "You've been with us for five hours. Why didn't you tell us you were a Kurd right away?" "We weren't alone." I got to know the driver and the young boy. "My name is Azad." "Heso," said the driver. "My name is Shivan, but for official purposes I have an Arabic name, Mohammed," said the young boy, smiling. "How did you persuade the officer to give me my papers and let me go?" "I traffic with him. I know his secrets."

I took out some money to pay my fare. He refused to accept at first, but then he said, "Because you're a tourist, which means you have money. Otherwise . . ."

The young boy kept looking at me and repeating, "We're Kurds, right? We're brothers, right? We'll be free, right?"

I still had my little bag on my lap with the Kurdish suit, the cassette of Kurdish music, and the book of Kurdish poetry. The driver opened the glove compartment and took out a cassette, which he slipped into the player. It was the voice of Mahmad Shekho, the tall, skinny Kurd from Syria. It was the same song I'd heard in the refugee camp in Iran in

1974. The car swung onto a road that cut far into the distance through an immense plain.

"The more time goes by, the more my heart beats slowly, my beloved . . ."

As for me, Azad, I was no longer a kid.

AZAD lived in Italy for many years, but couldn't obtain a residency card because Italy did not recognize Kurds as having official refugee status. He settled in France.

SHERO SELIM MALAY, his father, died on December 18, 1996. His son couldn't attend his funeral because it was impossible for him to return to Kurdistan.

GENERAL BARZANI died of cancer in New Jersey in 1978.

HAYBET, Azad's mother, became blind in her left eye. She lives in Aqra in their fortress-house, alone.

ROSTAM, Azad's brother, fled in 1997. He is presently a refugee in Germany.

DILOVAN, Azad's other brother and Zilan's father, fought with the resistance groups in the mountains of Kurdistan. He is the father of eleven children. The parents of his wife, DIJLA, were killed by the chemicals used during the Anfal, Saddam Hussein's campaign to exterminate the Kurds between February 1987 and September 1988.

TAMAN, Azad's sister, lived in the concentration camps.

RAMO, Azad's cousin, studied architecture in Baghdad and died under torture in 1982.

CHETO, the cousin with the stunt pigeons, became an agricultural engineer and looks after his orchard.

JACOB, the math teacher, was executed by firing squad in 1981 in Mosul.

SAMI, the painter, was never seen again after he was taken away by the secret police. His parents believe his body was dissolved in sulfuric acid.

SADDAM HUSSEIN was president of Iraq and lived in his palace in Baghdad until 2003.

IMAD, the musician, became an excellent violinist. He fell in love with a woman he wasn't supposed to marry; they ran away, but were murdered by their families when they returned two years later.

GALAVEJ, Azad's cousin who got married on the day of Azad's departure, had a daughter. Galavej's husband vanished in 1980 during the Iran-Iraq War.

The father of Jian, the girl who gave Azad a flashlight, was executed by firing squad. The rest of her family was deported to the concentration camps in southern Iraq.

On April 9, 2003, the coalition forces that had entered Iraq on March 19 conquered Baghdad, and Saddam Hussein's regime was toppled.